KNOWLEDGE STEW

THE GUIDE TO THE MOST
INTERESTING FACTS IN THE WORLD

DANIEL GANNINGER

VOLUME 1

Knowledge Stew: The Guide to the Most Interesting Facts in the World

Volume 1 - Knowledge Stew Guide

ISBN: 1517413761
ISBN-13: 978-1517413767

Printed in the United States of America

For Fun Fact Seekers Everywhere

CONTENTS

INTRODUCTION

How many times have you just had to tell someone something interesting you heard or read? Or maybe you've just wondered how something got its start or where it came from, and you just had to find out the story behind it. I've had the same problem, and this was where *Knowledge Stew* was born.

In the pages that follow you'll find a plethora of facts from around the world, and the details behind those facts in a number of categories. Some are short, they just don't require much more explanation, some are long, and delve into a topic, and others are right in-between. They can be enjoyed on a plane, a train, a boat, or in a taxi, and they're just as good in a nice, comfy chair.

So sit back and relax, grab a spoon, and help yourself to large helping of *Knowledge Stew*. Enjoy!

Daniel Ganninger
Author

HISTORY AND ALL ITS MYSTERIES – PART 1

That's the Best They Could Do?

Sometimes it's hard for expectant parents to come up with a middle name for their new child. One famous example of this was President Harry S. Truman, whose middle name was really "S". His parents couldn't decide on a name and gave him the letter to honor both his paternal and maternal grandfathers, Anderson Shipp Truman and Solomon Young. He later signed his middle name with a period after the "S" even though it didn't mean anything. And we thought it might mean "Stan".

The Good 'Ole Stars and Stripes

The design of the American flag has varied over the years, and it has a long and colorful history, but what do you really know about the flag?

We all remember that the fifty stars of the American flag represent all fifty states, and the thirteen stripes represent the thirteen original colonies. We learned that in grade school (if you were awake for that lesson). But how did the colors of the flag end up being red, white, and blue? Why not green, purple, and gold? For one, that would make one ugly flag, and two, it just wouldn't make much sense.

There are a few theories on why the flag is the colors red, white, and blue. One theory is that red came from the British colors (the redcoats), white to represent secession from Great Britain, and blue with stars to represent the sky, or a new constellation. The most likely explanation for the flag's colors is that they were borrowed from the Union Jack flag of England, which is also red, white, and blue. In addition, the colors just look good together. But what do the colors mean?

Back in 1777, the Marine Committee of the Second Continental Congress set what the flag should look like. They didn't, however, give the colors any meaning. It wasn't until 1782, when Charles

Thomson, Secretary of the Continental Congress, presented the Seal of the United States to Congress. He said the red of the seal signified hardiness and valor, blue signified vigilance, perseverance, and justice, and white signified innocence and purity. This was accepted not only for the seal, but also for the flag. Over the years others have differed on the meaning behind the colors (red for blood spilled in defending the nation and/or gaining independence, for example).

Before 1912, the flag had many different designs. The makers of the flags had unusual arrangements of the stars, and the flag was not a uniform size. It wasn't until an Executive Order by President Taft in 1912 established the proportions of the flag with stars in horizontal rows with the points of the stars pointing upwards. Stars were added to the flag as states were added to the United States after this time.

President Eisenhower made two executive orders in 1959 that established the flag as we know it today. The first was in an arrangement of seven rows of seven stars to allow for Alaska's admittance to the Union, and then later in 1959, he signed another executive order that put nine rows of stars horizontally and eleven rows of stars vertically, allowing Hawaii, the last state to be admitted, to get their spot on the flag.

There are many interesting facts about the flag; how it should be flown, where it should be flown, how it should be folded and stored, rules about its use, and so on. There are complete books on just these items. But one interesting question is; where can the flag be displayed twenty-four hours a day, 365 days a year?

There aren't as many places as you would think, at least not according to the letter of the law. All the places a flag can be flown day and night, 365 days a year, either had a presidential proclamation attached to them, or they had a public law that was passed giving them permission to do so. Of course, there probably are some other places that do fly the flag all the time, but these places don't have a specific law or presidential proclamation to do so. Here's the list of those places with a proclamation or law attached to flying the flag all the time:

The White House
The Washington Monument
The United States Marine Corps Memorial (Iwo Jima)

Flag House Square (Baltimore, Maryland)
Fort McHenry National Monument and Historic Shrine
(Baltimore, Maryland)
On the Green of the town of Lexington (Massachusetts)
United States Customs Ports of Entry
Grounds of the National Memorial Arch (Valley Forge State
Park, Pennsylvania)

Now, where is one more place that the flag flies twenty-four hours a day, seven days a week? Give up? It's on the Moon. There are six flags on the moon, and all but one is still standing. The first one set, by Neil Armstrong and Buzz Aldrin, is no longer upright. Aldrin confirmed they had placed the flag too close to the lunar module and blew it away as they lifted from the lunar surface. Bummer, huh?

Another bummer is that the flags still on the moon no longer look like American flags. They have become plain, old, white flags after being blasted over the years by intense UV rays and changes between hot and cold on the moon's surface. What do you expect from flags that were made from nylon in New Jersey in 1969 for a mere $5.50 apiece? Five continue to not wave in the vacuum of space but are still standing. Even though you can't tell they're American flags, it seems to have been not such a bad return on the investment, don't you think?

And the Award For Persistence Goes to...

Hiroo Onoda hid in the jungles of the Philippines for 29 years after the end of World War II because he didn't know, or didn't believe, the war was finally over. Onoda hid in the jungle with four other soldiers and continued to carry out guerilla activities. One of the soldiers surrendered in 1950 while another was shot and killed in 1954.

Onoda and the other remaining soldier, Shoichi Shimada, were in the jungle for another eighteen years before Shimada was killed in 1972 by local police after the pair continued conducting guerilla activities in the area. Onoda finally emerged in 1974 and formally surrendered to Philippine President Ferdinand Marcos. He was even still wearing his 30-year-old imperial Japanese uniform. But he only gave his formal surrender when his former commander from 1945 flew to the country and reversed his orders. He died in 2014 at the age of 91 in Japan.

The Most Studied Artifact in History

The Shroud of Turin is a centuries old linen cloth that appears to be a crucified man, believed by many to be that of Jesus Christ. It has become the single most studied artifact in human history. The amount of research on the cloth has been mind boggling, being studied for hundreds of thousands of hours. But the controversy continues.

One such bit of controversy relates to the carbon dating of the shroud. A piece of the shroud was split and tested in laboratories in Switzerland, England, and the United States in 1988. The carbon-14 dating placed the cloth in the time frame between 1260 to 1390 A.D. The conclusion of the scientists was that the shroud was a medieval hoax.

But a 2013 analysis by Italian scientists revealed that the part of the cloth that had been tested may have come from a portion of the shroud that had been repaired by an order of nuns after it had been damaged in a fire during the Middle Ages. Their research using infrared light and spectroscopy dated the shroud between 280 B.C. to 220 A.D.

The shroud has been moved, transferred, displayed, and handled extensively since the 1300s, so it may be no small surprise that definitive answers to its origin have been hard to come by. It's such a complex research piece that it would be impossible to cover all of it in this tiny space, and each new piece of research seems to only open up more questions. One of the most basic questions still doesn't have a consensus. Scientists have no idea how the image even got fixed to the cloth.

The shroud is currently housed at the Cathedral of Saint John the Baptist in Turin, Italy and is in an airtight, bulletproof container that also keeps out ambient light. It is controlled for humidity and temperature, and the inside of the container is composed of 95% argon gas, and 0.5% oxygen to preserve the piece.

Don't Be So Superstitious

Are you superstitious? Do you avoid black cats or maybe toss some salt over your shoulder when you want to ward off a bit of bad luck? In that case, you might have the heebie-jeebies, or you might just be a little strange. Don't worry, superstitions are rooted in history, and they all have a back story. Hey, we've all done them once in a while.

Knock On Wood – This superstition is commonly used after we say something we hope doesn't come to pass, such as, "I've never lost my wallet—knock on wood." The origins are ancient, probably starting back in Greece or with the Native Americans.

These cultures regarded trees as places where the gods lived. It's believed that if a person boasted of some sort of success, such as in battle, they would knock on the wood of a tree to calm the god contained inside so the god wouldn't be angry about the boast. Another origin could have originated from the Christians who touched wooden crosses to ask forgiveness from some misdeed, or to ensure safety from, or against, a particular misfortune.

Four-leaf clover – The origin of the four-leaf clover was believed to have come from the Druids of the British Isles, an ancient Celtic priesthood. They held rituals in oak groves that involved collecting rare four-leaf clovers and mistletoe. It was believed these things helped the Druids see into the future.

The Romans tried to eliminate Druidism, as did the Christians. This may have elevated their cult status even more, thus putting the four-leaf clover into a mythical realm. The religion ended when the Celts were Christianized, but the clover's shape as a cross probably helped further its popularity. The rate of finding a four-leaf clover in the wild is 1 in 10,000, so good luck in finding one. That Druid ritual must have been one time-consuming affair.

Black Cats – Don't cross a black cat's path or you'll get bad luck. Sure, cats seem to urinate on everything and are sometimes moody as hell, but they have been revered throughout history. The Egyptians kept them as honored pets and would often mummify them, as did people in the Far East.

After the Medieval Ages the cat population increased around the time of fear over witches and witchcraft. A stray black cat was just naturally associated with some evil power, and since black magic and a black cat seem to go together, an irrational fear was formed.

France even started to try to eradicate the felines in the 1600s after England had been swept up in black cat mania. What was the cure from folklore if you happened to cross the path of a black cat? Walk in a circle, go back to the spot where the black cat crossed your path, and count to thirteen. The poor black cats couldn't catch a break.

Walking Under a Ladder – This one is pretty simple—walk under a ladder and you get bad luck. If you just had to walk under a ladder, you were supposed to cross your fingers, spit after going under, and then not talk until you saw a dog. But where did this craziness come from?

In ancient Egypt, ladders were actually considered good luck. Ladders were found in tombs because of the belief that a ladder allowed the pharaohs the ability to climb to heaven. In addition, the triangle a ladder made represented the trinity of the gods, hence the pyramids. It was believed that if a common person walked under a triangular arch, they were committing an act against the gods. Think of it as trampling on their turf. A ladder against a wall would form this type of space, thus a no-no to go under.

Christians kept the superstition going. A ladder against the crucifix represented those that killed Jesus Christ. The ladder came to be a symbol of death and evil. Even in England in the 1600s, criminals about to be hanged had to walk under the ladder of the gallows while executioners walked around it.

Broken Mirror, Seven Years Bad Luck – The origins of this superstition are believed to have begun in ancient Greece when people would go to see a type of fortune teller called a "mirror seer". This person would examine a reflection and tell the person's fortune, or misfortune, if it came to that.

The Romans put their own spin on the superstition since they believed a person's health cycled every seven years. A broken mirror couldn't reflect a clear image of the person, so it came to mean seven years of misfortune, or bad luck.

Spilled salt – Everyone knows this one. If you spill some salt, you have to throw it over your left shoulder to avoid bad luck. This one is rooted in ancient times, back to the age of the Sumerians more than 5,500 years ago. Salt has always been a religious symbol (salt of the earth), and was considered a valuable commodity in ancient times. It's believed that throwing salt over your shoulder wards off evil omens, or smacks the salt into the face of the devil.

The Number 13 – The fear of the number 13 is also known by the word triskaidekaphobia, but everyone knew that. It's still very much engrained in our modern culture. High-rise buildings don't have a 13th floor (over 80% don't), some airports don't have a gate 13, and some hospitals don't have a room 13.

The origins of this insanity can possibly be traced back to a Norse myth. Twelve gods decided to have a dinner party in Valhalla. Another unwanted guest decides to crash the party—Loki (yes, the same god from the Thor comics and the 13th guest at this party). Loki somehow gets the god of darkness, Hoder, to shoot Balder, the god of joy. Balder kicks the bucket, and the earth is plunged into darkness. Sounds like fun, huh?

The Christians ran with it next, and the story fit nicely into the story of the last supper. Judas was the last disciple to show up, making 13. Judas betrays Jesus the next day—enough said. The Romans also got in on the act and believed covens were made of 12 witches with the 13th member being the devil, while the Egyptians believed there were 12 stages of life and the 13th stage was the afterlife, thus the association with death.

Another problem for the number 13 is that it comes behind 12. 12 can be divided equally, was the number of the disciples of Jesus, the months of the year, signs of the zodiac, gods of Olympus, tribes of Israel, and members of a jury. To be 13 just doesn't add up right. It's believed that approximately 17 to 21 million Americans have a fear of the number 13, especially on Fridays.

Good Luck Horseshoe – This is a common good luck charm and is believed to come from the fact that a horseshoe has seven holes (seven being a lucky number), and made of iron, which supposedly wards off evil spirits.

There is some disagreement on whether the horseshoe should face up or down. The up camp contends that this holds the luck in and protects everything around it. The down camp contends that the luck spills down on whoever is fortunate enough to walk under it. Which do you prefer? My preference would be that the horseshoe is secured well enough that when I do walk under it, it doesn't have the chance to knock me out.

Fascinating Facts About the 4th of July

Since July 4th, 1776, Independence Day has been a celebration recognizing the birth of American independence. We all know that, but what are some other interesting facts about the holiday that may have escaped you? Some of them may surprise you.

A brief refresher in history is in order to remember how the holiday even came about. It all started with that little thing called the American Revolution. Thirteen representatives of the colonies fighting in the war met in June of 1776 to decide about declaring their independence from Great Britain.

On June 7th, 1776, there was a heated debate on the issue. The Continental Congress was unable to come to an agreement on a resolution introduced by Richard Henry Lee representing Virginia. A vote was postponed and a five member committee was formed to draft a document that would justify the colonial break with Great Britain. The group consisted of Thomas Jefferson, John Adams, Benjamin Franklin, Roger Sherman, and Robert R. Livingston.

On July 2nd, 1776, the Continental Congress voted for independence unanimously (but it took New York a little time to vote in agreement). On July 4th the delegates adopted the Declaration of Independence. Now that the history lesson is out of the way, we can get on to some interesting facts about Independence Day.

Even though the vote for independence took place on July 2nd, the holiday was recognized to occur on July 4th. The reason was because the document wasn't completely written and printed until the 4th.

John Adams believed the July 2nd date was the actual date of independence and protested the July 4th date by not accepting invitations to events on that day.

The Liberty Bell didn't ring on July 4th, 1776. It was rung instead on July 8, 1776 to mark the first public reading of the Declaration of Independence.

Some colonist held mock funerals of King George III to represent the break from the monarchy during celebrations of the day.

The first official holiday was held on July 4th, 1777. The new nation was still at war, but Congress authorized the use of fireworks in celebrating the holiday.

George Washington gave double rations of rum to the soldiers to mark the holiday in 1778.

Massachusetts became the first state to make July 4th an official state holiday in 1781.

Three U.S. presidents have died on the holiday. John Adams and Thomas Jefferson both died just a few hours apart on July 4, 1826— the 50 year anniversary of the signing of the Declaration of Independence—and James Monroe died on July 4th, 1831.

The U.S. didn't make July 4th a federal holiday until 1870.

In 1941, Congress approved July 4th as a paid holiday to federal employees. It is one of only four federal holidays that are celebrated each year. The others? Christmas Day, New Year's Day, and Thanksgiving Day.

More than 14,000 firework displays occur each July 4th across the country.

The largest fireworks display is Macy's Fourth of July Spectacular in New York City. The display uses 75,000 lbs of fireworks and lasts about thirty minutes. The celebration is attended by approximately 2 million people.

The July 4th weekend has always been a gastronomical event, but the effects of how much food and beverages are consumed can stick with people well after the celebrations. Here's a reason why, and hold on to your stomach.

It's estimated that 150 million hot dogs are consumed during the July 4th holiday. That's roughly 18 million pounds of hotdogs. But buns are needed, so that requires 18.75 million packages of 8-count buns to cradle those hot dogs.

Now, after consuming all those hot dogs, how much did people eat? A hot dog is approximately 137 calories, so around 20.55 billion calories are consumed of just hot dogs (buns excluded) during the celebrations on July 4th. A good walk or run on a treadmill is definitely in order.

Unexpected Aviators

In France in 1783, a rooster, sheep, and a duck became the world's first hot-air balloon passengers. Each type of animal was used for a specific reason. The sheep was the animal that most closely resembled a human's physiology. The duck was used as a control since it already flew at altitude and was believed that it wouldn't be harmed during the flight. And the rooster was added since it was a bird that did not fly at high altitude and could be used to test the effects of altitude.

The flight took place at the royal palace of Versailles and lasted about eight minutes and went up to around 1,500 feet. Interestingly, the sheep was named Montauciel, meaning "climb to the sky".

An Unfortunate Mistake

A bible printed in 1631, often called the "Wicked Bible", had the line, "Thou shalt commit adultery" included in the text. The printers forgot to include the word "not". They were fined and had their printing license revoked. This particular edition is also sometimes called the Adulterous, or Sinners' Bible.

The printers who made the mistake were the royal printers in London and were fined 300 pounds, or about $43,586 in today's dollars. Charles I and the Archbishop of Canterbury, George Abbott, were of course beside themselves. The copies were immediately burned, except for the few that exist today. In 2010, a copy of the Wicked Bible was offered for the low, low price of $89,500 and supposedly was sold.

Copies of the "Wicked Bible" still reside in the New York Library's rare book collection, the British Library in London, and another is in the Dunham Bible Museum in Houston, Texas.

The 1962 Fire That Never Stops

There's a fire that burns in the United States underground, right now, and has been doing so for over 50 years. What's even harder to fathom is that this fire could burn for another 250 years. I'm talking about the Centralia mine fire in Pennsylvania, a disaster that first took place in 1962.

Since that time in '62, a coal seam in the Centralia mine has been on fire at depths up to 300 feet. The fire is eight-miles in length, and covers 3,700 acres, all underground. The cause is largely unknown, but there are a number of hypotheses on how it started. The most common explanation is that burning trash ignited a coal seam in a cave which caused the massive fire.

Back in 1962, the Centralia City Council had the intention of cleaning up the town's landfill that was located in a previously cut strip mine. It had been proposed as a way to stop the problem of illegal dumping which had sprung up around the area. Ironically, I guess, the State of Pennsylvania had passed a law in 1956 that regulated landfills used in strip mines because of the danger of fire from a mine.

An inspector from the state even informed a councilman that the pit would need to be filled with some type of incombustible material when he saw that the landfill had developed holes in the walls and ground. It's unknown why, but instead of filling the landfill with incombustible material, the council decided to set the landfill on fire to clean it up. They hired a fire crew to do the job on May 17, 1962, and a fire was started.

The crew was able to extinguish the fire that night, but more flames were seen on May 29 as well as on June 4th. They tried moving the garbage with a bulldozer to get at the layers that could still be on fire, but what was discovered a few days later was a 15 foot-wide hole that had been hidden where garbage had accumulated. It was believed this hole may have led to the old tunnels of the mine and the combustible coal seam. Even with all of this going on, the council continued to allow dumping in the landfill.

Things became serious when holes that had smoke coming from them were tested and found to have carbon monoxide amounts that were consistent with those in other mine fires. Lethal levels of carbon monoxide were found on August 9th, and all mines in the area were closed. An early attempt at excavating the site was done shortly thereafter, but once other mine chambers were opened to get to the fire, the influx of oxygen only fueled it further. Eventually the project ran out of money and had to be stopped because the crews couldn't keep up with the growing fire that was now going deeper.

A second attempt at extinguishing the fire was made in November of 1962, with the idea of filling the mine and snuffing out the fire with crushed rock mixed with water that would be pumped into the areas of the mine ahead of the known fire. Funding ran out again in March of 1963, and because of a cold, snowy winter, the ability of the company to fill the area was substantially affected. By this time in 1963, the fire had already spread 700 feet from where it was believed to have started.

It wasn't until 1979 when the locals began to discover that the problem was much greater than they had realized. In 1981, the problem came to a head when a 12 year-old boy named Todd Domboski fell part-way into a 4-foot wide sinkhole that was 150-feet deep which had opened up in his backyard. Luckily, he was saved by his cousin who pulled him to safety. The steam coming from the sinkhole had carbon monoxide that was measured to be at lethal levels. The town of Centralia had a serious problem, and a deadly one at that.

The U.S. Congress in 1984 allocated more than $42 million for the relocation of the Centralia area residents. Most residents left, but some chose to stay. In 1992, the Pennsylvania governor used the power of eminent domain to condemn all the buildings. A legal fight followed by some of the residents, but it failed. The U.S. Postal Service revoked the zip code of Centralia in 2002, and in 2012 the last remaining residents were ordered to leave after they lost their appeal in court. Seven residents were allowed to stay in 2013 to live out their lives, after which their properties would be taken through eminent domain.

These were the only people left from the population of 2,761 people that lived in the town in 1980. But Centralia wasn't the only casualty of the mine fire. The nearby town of Byrnesville also had to be abandoned and leveled to the ground.

The Centralia mine is believed to have enough fuel to burn for another 250 years as it continues to follow the vast coal seam and tunnels underground. Temperatures inside the heart of the fire are believed to be more than 1,000 degrees Fahrenheit and contain a lethal mix of carbon monoxide and other gases. Even with the deadly fumes and danger, Centralia has become a tourist attraction as people go to see a fire that can't be stopped and a town that has disappeared.

Who Thought This Would Be a Good Idea?

The U.S. chose 00000000 as the password for its computer controls of nuclear tipped missiles for nearly 20 years. Strange, but true. In 1962, John F. Kennedy signed the National Security Action Memorandum 160, which authorized that nuclear weapons had to have something called a Permissive Action Link, or PAL. This was a security device for the weapons that would prevent unauthorized arming or detonation.

The reason for the PAL was to ensure that if some other government got hold of the nukes they wouldn't be able to launch them. It was also in place so that U.S. military commanders couldn't launch a nuke all by themselves and so they would never be in the control of one person. The problem occurred, as it often does with anything dealing with the government, that the military simply neglected to fit the PALs to many of the nuclear devices, and they were instead secured only by mechanical locks. The ones that were fit with the PAL, such as the Minuteman Silos in the U.S., were done so under the Secretary of Defense for Kennedy, Robert McNamara.

When he left, the Strategic Air Command, which oversees most of the United States nuclear military strike force, changed the codes to 00000000. This extremely easy code was even written on a checklist so no one would forget. The reasons were twofold; there would no need for presidential approval if there was an attack, and if the lines of communication had been destroyed , there would still be the ability to launch the missiles. Under the Strategic Air Commands thinking, this ensured that launching nuclear missiles would be quick and easy.

Now, don't you feel better that almost anyone had the capability of launching nuclear weapons?

Left or Right? Why Some Countries Drive on the Other Side of the Road

About 65% of the world drives on the right side of the road. Everyone else drives on the left. What is the origin of driving on the left side of the road, and are they right or wrong?

Countries that continue to drive on the left side of the road are mainly those places that used to be British colonies. In the medieval days, most people used the left side of the road. It had to do with safety and security, and the avoidance of getting killed. Anyone with a sword preferred the left side of the road. This enabled the swordsman to keep their right arm close to an opponent and their sword away from them on the other side. In addition, a horse is easier to mount from the left side for a right-handed person. It just made good sense. A rider could mount their horse on the side of the road instead of in the middle where they could clog up traffic and make the peasant folk angry. So how did it change to the right?

The shift can be traced back to the 1700s when teams would haul farm products to market pulled by several horses. The products were carried in large wagons and the driver would ride the rear horse on the left. This allowed him to drive the team with his right arm while keeping an eye out as people passed on the left. It also allowed the driver of the team to make sure he didn't run into other wagons.

In 1752, Empress Elizabeth of Russia officially declared that traffic must keep to the right, as was the custom for the country at the time. The practice became more widespread in 1789 during the French Revolution. An official rule for right-side driving was made in Paris in 1794.

There was an interesting reason for this change. Before the revolution, aristocracy traveled on the left-side of the road, forcing peasants to the right. Later on, the aristocracy began using the right-side of the road to blend in with the peasants, thus cementing France's drive to the right. Denmark was the next major country to follow and adopted the right-side rule in 1793.

Napoleon spread driving on the right further. As he conquered different countries, they were forced to adopt the right-side rule. Only the countries that had denied Napoleon's attacks kept their left-side of the road rules.

The United Kingdom persevered throughout it all and kept their left-side road driving. They made it official and mandatory in 1835. All the countries in the British Empire followed this same rule. After the breakup of the British Empire, all of the countries that had been former British colonies kept the left-side rule except for Egypt, which had been conquered by Napoleon before the British got there. Napoleon even got the Dutch to drive on the right when he conquered the Netherlands, but their colonies continued to drive on the left.

In early America, since it was a British colony, the driving custom was on the left. It wasn't until the American Revolution when Americans wanted to cut all ties with Britain that they began driving on the right. Even in Canada there was a divide. The French portion drove on the right, and the British areas drove on the left. It wasn't until the 1920s before most of Canada agreed on the right side, with the exception of Newfoundland, which joined Canada in 1949.

Over the years, countries in Europe slowly began to change due to influences from World War II and the pervasiveness of the American car, which had the steering wheel on the left. Only four European countries remain with left-side driving; the United Kingdom, Malta, Cyprus, and Ireland. The United Kingdom even played around with the idea of switching to the right in the 1960s, but they discovered it would be cost prohibitive and the political pressures to remain on the left were too great.

Some Great Bonus Facts About Driving on the Left

There have been only three countries that have gone from right to left side driving. East Timor did it in 1975, Okinawa in 1978, and Somoa in 2009, mainly because they wanted to import cheaper cars from the left-side driving countries of Australia, New Zealand, and Japan.

In Myanmar they drove on the left until 1970 when General Ne Win, the ruler at the time, ordered everyone to the right. What was interesting was that he supposedly got the advice to do so from a wizard. The problem was, most every vehicle in the country had a right-sided steering wheel, and there are still old traffic lights in Rangoon that are on the wrong side of the road.

If you plan to drive in the Bahamas, where they drive on the left, don't be surprised if you get a rental car with a left-side steering wheel. Due to its location near the United States, many of the cars there are American made. That makes for some interesting driving, as some people have reported.

It's legal to drive a right-sided steering car in the U.S. as long as it has the necessary registrations and passes all the American laws and regulations in place for that particular car.

In the U.S. you can buy and drive a right-sided steering postal vehicle but only when it has been retired from service.

Glad They Didn't Use Something Else

The death of the pope used to be confirmed by striking him on the forehead three times with a small silver hammer while calling out his name. Striking is probably not the most accurate of words, it was probably more of a tap, but the process was used for Pope Paul VI's death in 1978. It may have been ceremonially done upon the death of

Pope John Paul II in 2005, but Vatican doctors officially used an electrocardiogram to determine that he was indeed deceased. The Vatican also released the death certificate of Pope John Paul II, something they had never done before.

The silver hammer ceremony is an old ceremony and has always been carefully laid out. Upon the pope's death, there is one cardinal who becomes known as the Camerlengo of the Universal Church. He is in charge of the interim government of the church before a new pope is elected. The camerlengo is the one who uses the silver hammer on the pope.

In the case of Pope Paul VI, the camerlengo had Vatican officials, two other cardinals, and Italian representatives watch as he tapped the forehead of the pope three times and said his name, while asking if he was dead. With confirmation that the Pope is deceased, the camerlengo locks the private apartment of the pope, and the papal secretary draws up the death certificate. The camerlengo, who is now in charge of all Vatican affairs, along with a committee of cardinals, begin the summoning process that will bring all the cardinals to the Vatican to convene a conclave where the new pope will be elected.

ONE WITH NATURE

The Most Perfect Storm

There is a curious weather phenomenon that occurs which is almost as consistent as Old Faithful in Yellowstone National Park. Thunderstorm Hector, or "Hector the Convector" as it's sometimes known, is a thundercloud that forms nearly every day on the Tiwi Islands, Northern Territory, Australia, and reaches heights of 66,000 ft. Scientists are befuddled as to why it occurs. It's always funny to see a befuddled scientist.

That's Just Shocking

Lightning strikes the earth about 8 million times a day, and a lightning bolt generates temperatures five times hotter than those found at the sun's surface. That's about 53,540 degrees Fahrenheit compared to 10,340 degrees at the sun's surface, just in case anyone is wondering. The air around a lightning bolt heats the air to around 18,000 degrees Fahrenheit, and this causes the air to expand rapidly. This produces the sound wave we know as thunder.

When You Get That Sinking Feeling

Mexico City is sinking at a rate of 18 inches per year. Unfortunately, the Aztecs built the city in the middle of a lake that had formed in a volcanic crater. As the city continued to grow, the soil compacted and the water was removed from the underground aquifer, further adding to the problem.

How Sweet It Is

There's an interesting substance contained in licorice root. It's called glycyrrhizin, and it's 30 times sweeter than table sugar. Licorice root has been used for thousands of years in both Eastern and Western medicine for treating everything from the common cold to liver disease. It's also a common flavoring in tobacco. Who knew?

A Different Sort of Egg

The Araucana chicken of Chile lays blue eggs. The egg color is believed to have evolved because of a DNA retrovirus that happened at some time during the chicken's domestication. The eggs aren't any healthier, or unhealthier, than regular eggs. One advantage for the egg is that it is already blue, making eggs for Easter a snap. Just make sure to cook it first.

Where Have All the Fireflies Gone?

Fireflies were once a sign of summer, their little buttocks glowing in the night, but they are becoming almost impossible to find nowadays. Where have they gone, and what has made them disappear?

Catching fireflies has always been a summer ritual. You could run through a field or find them in your backyard. It became a fun game to chase and collect as many as you could, just to watch them glow. But something strange has happened. Fireflies aren't around as much anymore, at least not in the numbers that many remember as a kid. Sure there are sightings in certain areas, but nothing as prolific as twenty to thirty years ago. There may be two reasons for the decline in the firefly population—development and light pollution.

Most fireflies start out in fields, marshes, or forests, and they seldom ever leave. They're like that old guy in the house down the street; he's been there forever and has no plans to leave until his kids force him out. Fireflies develop as larvae in rotting wood and near streams and ponds. There are many different species of fireflies, and each one thrives in a different environment. Some fireflies like the forest while others prefer fields or streams.

As you know, development around the country has increased, but with the increase, the habitat of the firefly is being taken over.

As more and more development occurs, the home-bodied fireflies are getting snuffed out.

Another possible reason for the decline in fireflies is the increase in light pollution. Scientists don't know for sure, but human light may influence the firefly's ability to communicate. Both females and male fireflies use their flashes of light to communicate, warn off predators, defend their territory, and to attract a mate. It may be the case that the fireflies just can't find each other anymore. Their signals could be drowned out because of excess light in their habitats. Unfortunately, fireflies don't have an online dating service to find each other.

Fireflies, or otherwise known as lightning bugs, are winged beetles. There are over 2,000 species of fireflies, and the larvae are often called "glow worms". They produce a light that has no infrared or ultraviolet frequencies. The light occurs because of bioluminescence and takes place in specialized organs, usually on the abdomen of the firefly. A light emitting compound called luciferin, in the presence of oxygen, adenosine triphosphate, and magnesium, causes light to be emitted when acted on by the enzyme luciferase. This bioluminescence can be red, green, or yellow. It's nature's rock-n-roll light show.

Fireflies are small and amazing creatures, and only time will tell how their habitats will be ultimately affected. One thing is for certain, it would be a bummer if they no longer light up the sky on those warm summer nights.

A Bird That Needs to Check In With Air Traffic Control

In 1973, a Ruppell's griffon vulture, the planet's highest flying bird, was reportedly ingested by an airliner's jet engine as it cruised over Abidjan, Cote d'Ivoire in Africa at 36,100 feet. This is an amazing feat, and the altitude is much higher than Mt. Everest (29,029 ft).

These birds commonly fly at about 20,000 ft, and they a high affinity for oxygen that allows them to fly at these extreme levels. The vultures have a variant of hemoglobin alphaD that allows them to breathe despite the low partial pressure of the upper atmosphere. They are the only animal known to survive and function at such incredible heights. It would be interesting to know what the evolutionary advantage there is to having this ability. It could allow for greater range in travel as it takes advantage of the upper winds, or it may be because there are no other predators that would be able to take them out of the sky; except for man-made airplanes of course.

You Don't Want to Meet One of These in a Dark Alley

The honey badger is listed in the Guinness Book of World Records as the "World's Most Fearless Creature". The honey badger is found in Southwest Asia, Africa, and the Indian Subcontinent and is a member of the weasel family, but they don't act like weasels. Honey badgers are known for their strength and ferocity. They have been known to attack almost any type of animal when threatened. Their skin is thick, and the animals have an almost tireless endurance capacity during confrontations.

I Wonder If Elephants Can Smell Themselves?

Elephants have many remarkable abilities, and one of the most impressive is that elephants can smell water several miles away. An elephant's smelling ability is the greatest among any mammals, research has found, even eclipsing the incredible smelling sense of the bloodhound.

The elephant's trunk contains five times more smell receptors than a human's nose, and they are contained in the elephant's upper nasal cavity, where there are millions of the receptor cells. The elephant can wave its trunk in the air to collect air samples which are then transmitted to its extensive sensory system to determine not only the direction of the water, but also how far away it is. An elephant's memory isn't the only thing fascinating about this animal.

There's a Reason it's the National Bird

In 1782, the bald eagle was chosen as the National Emblem of the United States, but that isn't the only remarkable thing about this bird.

A bald eagle uses its feathers for balance, and if it loses a feather on one side, it will lose the same feather on the other side to remain perfectly balanced.

Bald eagles have over 7,000 feathers that are extremely lightweight but very strong. They are made of keratin, the same substance that makes up their talons and beak. It's also the same substance that makes up human fingernails and toenails. Just like fingernails, an eagle's new feather will push out an old one as it grows.

If you ever find an eagle feather, don't even think about keeping it. It's against the law and illegal to possess any part of an eagle. You're required to give any parts, feathers included, over to the proper authorities.

Take a Swim and Get Rich

There is so much gold in the ocean (about 20 million tons) that every person on earth could have 9 pounds of it. Unfortunately, each liter of seawater only contains 13 billionths of a gram of gold, so the concentration is miniscule. There is gold in the seafloor, but it's deep in rock beneath the ocean floor one or two miles underwater. No one has been able to come up with a cost efficient way to mine it from the ocean yet. Maybe you'll be the first one to come up with a plan. Good Luck!

No Need to Offer Them a Drink

Kangaroo rats are so incredibly adapted to desert life that they can go their whole lives without a single drink of water. How can they do that you ask? Kangaroo rats live in underground burrows where they have a supply of seeds.

Each night, usually for about 15 minutes per day, they gather more seeds that they carry in expandable pouches in their cheeks. They even make sure the outside of the seeds are dried before they store them away in their burrows. The kangaroo rat has very efficient kidneys and has some of the most concentrated urine of any North

American mammal. Due to this efficiency, they can get most of the moisture they need to survive from the inside of the seeds they eat.

IT'S JUST BUSINESS, MONEY, AND WORK

Lawyers, Lawyers, They're Everywhere

Have you ever wondered why there are so many lawyer commercials during the day on television? It's because two-thirds of the world's lawyers live in the United States. I guess that explains some things. It might also explain why we love to sue, and why Congress seems so inept.

In 2011, new law degrees came in at around 44,000 for the year. Thirty-five years ago, new law degrees were being produced at the rate of 34,000 per year. The overall number of lawyers back then was over 450,000. Today that number stands at 1.22 million.

With all this growth, the bubble may be bursting. Jobs in an actual law firm are now hard to come by. Online legal advice and tools are subverting the need to seek an attorney's advice or pay attorney's fees, and the median salary of a new lawyer has dropped dramatically. Some students must be getting the picture that we are up to our eyeballs in lawyers because since 2012, there has been an 11% decrease in the enrollment of first year law students.

Everything from A to Z

Amazon.com, the largest retailer in the world, made $74.45 billion in revenue for 2013. Yes, that's billion, with a "b", and that is more than the GDP (Gross Domestic Product) of over half the countries in the world. With that being said, Amazon didn't burn up the track in actual income. It only made $274 million in profit during 2013 after losing $39 million the year before in 2012. Here are some amazing facts about the company that serves over 137 million customers, a week.

How It All Got Started – Jeff Bezos, the founder and current CEO of Amazon, started the company in his garage in Seattle in 1994. He originally wanted to call the company "Cadabra", but his lawyer thought he wanted to call it "cadaver". Bezos came up with the name Amazon instead, to indicate the large size of what was offered, and also to ensure his company's name would come up first in website listings (as they were categorized back then).

The Iconic Logo – The logo for the company, as we have all seen, has the word "Amazon" with a smiling mouth going from the "A" to the "Z" in the name. This was to convey the point that the company would deliver anything, anywhere, from "A" to "Z".

The First Shipment – The first item Bezos sold from his garage was in 1995, and was a book titled, *Fluid Concepts & Creative Analogies: Computer Models of the Fundamental Mechanisms of Thought.* A man named John Wainwright bought that first book and even has a building at the South Lake Union Amazon campus called the Wainwright Building named after him.

The Reach of Amazon – Amazon controls over 10% of the all e-commerce in North America. Staples, Wal-Mart, Office Depot, Dell, Apple, Liberty, and Sears all share 10% together. The remaining retailers must fight for the left over 80%.

The Size – Everything at Amazon is done on a huge scale. Its S3 Cloud Platform could store 82 books for every person on earth. Even the warehouses of Amazon are grand. The company has 80 distribution centers, and the largest one could hold 28 football fields inside. They also use 1,400 Kiva Systems robots throughout the company to move product in the warehouses. Even when things don't go as planned they're huge. Once, in 2012, the Amazon site went down. In that time, the company missed out on about $5.7 million dollars in sales.

The Employees – Amazon even has an interesting take on customer service. Each employee of the company is required to spend two days every two years handling customer service calls so they can understand the customer service process.

The Future? – The future of Amazon is still not predictable. The company continues to invest heavily in its infrastructure and cites this as the reason for the low profits over the company's history. But Amazon doesn't seem to be ready to stop innovating, despite nervous investors. Bezos has already announced plans for a flying robotic delivery service. You never know anymore, one of those things might be depositing a smiling box on your doorstep in the near future.

A Quick Zipper Interlude

I just looked. It really is there. The YKK that is printed on your zipper stands for Yoshida Kogyo Kabushikikaisha, or YKK group. It's a group of Japanese manufacturing companies, and they are the world's largest zipper manufacturer.

Social Networking Sites You Thought Were Dead

Everyone seems to have a profile on Facebook, Twitter, Google +, Instagram—you get the idea. The possibilities never seem to stop. But what happened to all those great social networks that came before. Were they relegated to the dustbin of history, never to be seen or heard from again, or did they morph into something else? Their fate may leave a clue to the ultimate destiny of the current social networks.

It seems social media is always changing. Once one thing becomes popular there's something waiting eagerly in the wings to take over. Hopefully something better, something that improves the ability of someone to take a picture of a person in overly tight pants, paste a sarcastic message about said person and their pants, and then share that image and the snarky message to their throngs of friends and followers.

Well, there doesn't appear to be a major new social network coming on the horizon quite yet, but there were plenty from the not so distant past; the social networks that appeared to crash and burn, or were slowly forgotten. But did they really disappear?

Friendster – Friendster was an early social network before the time of the behemoth, Facebook. Friendster was founded in 2002 and was one of the first major social networks to have over 1 million members. The site even had an offer by Google in 2003 to buy it for $30 million. They turned the offer down.

By 2008, Friendster had 115 million users, but traffic began to decline starting in 2009. Friendster eventually lost all popularity in the U.S., mainly due to the rise in Facebook. At the end of 2009, Friendster was bought by the Asian internet giant, MOL Global. In June 2011, they rebranded themselves as a social gaming site in Asia and discontinued the social networking accounts. Friendster lasted three more years, and announced on June 14, 2015 that it was shutting down for good.

GeoCities – Remember when almost everybody had a personal website from GeoCities? The free service started in 1995 and became a hit rather quickly. It allowed internet users to have their own personal home page, and the users were referred to as "homesteaders". If you became a "homesteader" you picked one of the 14 GeoCities neighborhoods to reside in and were then assigned a number. That number actually became the users web address, or as GeoCities liked to call it, "street address".

The pages were usually a mix of mind-numbing colors, gaudy text, and computer driven music (those cool midi tracks) as people were getting their first taste of web design. Those GeoCities pages were likely the first spot where the everyday person could grab their own personal space on the web.

By June of 1997, the site was the fifth most popular site on the web, and the company went public a year later. By 1999, GeoCities had moved to the third spot of the most visited sites, only behind AOL and Yahoo. In that same year, Yahoo purchased GeoCities for $3.57 billion in stock, during the time of the dot-com bubble. After that time, GeoCities slowly began to fade.

By 2001, under rumors that the site was not making money, Yahoo introduced a fee program to host a page, and the free accounts were restricted. GeoCities as part of Yahoo somehow managed to bounce along for another eight years before Yahoo finally pulled the plug in 2009. Even though Yahoo shut it down in the U.S., you can still get a free page, but you'll have to move to Japan.

Usenet – Usenet, the earliest form of divulging information, was established in 1980. Usenet were newsgroups that covered every topic imaginable, all in text format. It was a precursor to the forums that we see today, largely without a moderator. In many ways it was like the wild, wild west of the internet.

Many terms we use today had their start on Usenet. The term "spamming" was one of them. Usenet was unregulated, but many important announcements were made through it. Usenet was an avenue to release information before information was readily available like it is today.

Usenet's initial decline is largely attributed to the "Eternal September", a term used to describe the time when AOL began offering access to the internet and to Usenet in 1993. Before that time, Usenet was largely used in colleges and universities. "Eternal September" denoted the time that incoming freshman would first access the network, and the large influx of new users who didn't understand the customs of using Usenet.

Usenet has all but died due to poor user numbers, and also because of its reputation for attracting the seedier underbelly of society. Most server companies or universities offering the newsgroups have shut them down. Duke University, where Usenet started with a connection to the University of North Carolina, shut down its Usenet server in May, 2010, thirty years after it started.

Second Life – Who would want to have a second life? Apparently many did and still do. Second Life was an online virtual world where users (or residents as they are called) can interact with each other as avatars. You can purchase or rent "virtual real estate", socialize, trade goods, and join in group activities. It even has its own currency. Sounds like a blast, huh?

Second Life started in 2003, and rose in popularity in 2005 and 2006 when it was learned people were making a living off of it, in a virtual world. Second Life peaked in 2009 and began a steady decline after that. Second Life is too complicated and confusing to try and explain how it works here, unless you've actually participated in it. As surprising as it is, Second Life is not dead. It's still alive and kicking with about 1 million users, and it can still be joined for free.

MySpace – Beside Friendster, MySpace probably had the biggest downfall because of Facebook. Viewing certain MySpace pages could almost put you in seizure-inducing fit. MySpace was actually born from employees of eUniverse, an internet marketing company, who had Friendster accounts. They started it in 2003 and used many of Friendster's popular features as part of MySpace. Most of the first accounts were eUniverse employees.

MySpace gained tremendously in popularity with teenagers and young adults after that time. In 2005, Mark Zuckerberg turned down an offer by MySpace CEO, Chris DeWolfe, to buy Facebook. Later in 2005, MySpace was purchased by News Corporation for $580 million.

In 2006, MySpace hit 100 million accounts, and by 2008 it was considered the leading social network. At one point in 2007, it was valued at $12 billion. The decline began right after the peak in 2008, when Facebook overtook MySpace in the rankings. One of the reasons believed for the decline in membership (other than Facebook) was that MySpace developed everything themselves and didn't allow outside development, while Facebook did.

The final nail came in 2011 when membership declined dramatically from 95 million users to 65 million users in twelve months. Traffic spiraled down by 44% in February of that year, and later that month MySpace was put up for sale. It was sold in June 2011, and the price was rumored to be $35 million. Quite the drop from the $580 million News Corp had paid for the site six years before.

MySpace has somehow stayed afloat and was relaunched in 2013 as a music centered site with the help of Justin Timberlake, who has an ownership stake in the company. As of January of 2015, MySpace reportedly has 50.6 million active users.

Social media continues to be an ever changing environment, but some of these companies never really went away, they just found a new niche. Only time will tell how the current social networks will survive, but I hope whoever takes the reins as the ultimate social network still allows snarky comments about the person in the overly tight pants.

And Now You Know

The WD in WD-40 stands for water displacement. Not only that, but the 40 literally means the 40th attempt at perfecting the product. Norm Larsen was trying to invent a formula to prevent corrosion by displacing water, and he succeeded on his 40th try. It was first used to protect the outer skin of the Atlas missile from corrosion and rust. Larsen made it into a consumer product in 1958, and in 1969, the company that made WD-40, the Rocket Chemical Company, renamed themselves after their only product—WD-40.

The Amazing History of Vaseline (aka Petroleum Jelly)

Chapped lips are uncomfortable and painful. Heck, anything that is chapped is never pleasant. On a cold, dry night, you may have reached for a jar of Vaseline to take care of the nuisance. But when you slathered the Vaseline on, did you ever wonder what the stuff was, exactly? If you peel off the label and read the ingredients there is usually only one listed under the drug facts—100% White PetrolatumUSP. "Okay," you say to yourself, "but what in the world is that?" Where did it come from and the why does this particular thing work so well? The answers to those questions are rather interesting.

Vaseline, or petroleum jelly, is used for just about everything. Chances are you have a jar of the stuff sitting in your medicine cabinet or drawer somewhere in your home. A plucky inventor saw the potential of the substance back when it was being discarded as a byproduct of oil production.

Robert Chesebrough had something happen that none of us would want—his job became obsolete. Chesebrough was a chemist and his job consisted of clarifying kerosene from the oil of sperm whales. Sounds like fun, but the fun finally ended when oil was discovered in Titusville, Pennsylvania. He didn't let his new found unemployment get him down and decided to travel to Titusville to figure out what new products could be made from the black stuff coming from the ground.

In 1859, while in the oil fields of Titusville, Chesebrough discovered something interesting. The oil workers there were using a substance to heal their cuts and burns. It was a residue that was removed from oil rig pumps called rod wax.

The rod wax was a nuisance to workers because it caused their equipment to malfunction. Chesebrough saw an opportunity and began to collect the black, waxy substance. He returned to Brooklyn and began the tedious process of refining the substance. He discovered that by distilling the thinner, lighter oils from the rod wax, he could produce a light-colored gel, and he patented the process in 1872.

Chesebrough began to demonstrate the process around New York by burning his skin with acid or on an open flame. He would then use his invention to show how the injuries would heal. It's not known if he was available for kid's parties. He opened his first factory in 1870, and called it Vaseline. It was a mix of the German word for water and the Greek word for oil with the scientific sounding ending of -ine. In 1987, the Chesebrough Manufacturing Company was purchased by Unilever.

Petroleum jelly is a mix of hydrocarbons and is flammable only when it's heated to a liquid. Its water-propelling properties make it very effective in sealing what it's put over (such as chapped lips, cuts, or burns) as well as keeping moisture in. The whiter the jelly, the more it has been refined. The USP after the White Petrolatum indicates the grade of the substance.

Now that you know what it is, what else can it be used for? Chesebrough was such a firm believer in the stuff that he claimed to eat a spoonful every day. Maybe we won't go that far, but it does have an endless reported supply of uses. Here are just a few.

1. Shine patent-leather shoes
2. Take out lipstick stains–put a little on the stain and wash whatever it was on.
3. Get chewing gum off of wood or any other surface - dab a little until the gum disintegrates.
4. Restore old leather
5. Lubricate rusty hinges or machinery, zippers, etc
6. Stop fungal growth on turtle shells (We all have that problem)

7. Rub on chicken combs to prevent frostbite
8. Use it on car battery terminals to prevent corrosion
9. Moisturize the paws of dogs
10. Use it to control split ends

Those are just a few of the uses. You may not have a turtle or a chicken to try it on, but I'm sure you could find something.

Who Is Barbie?

Ruth Handler got the idea for Barbie after watching her daughter, Barbara, play with paper dolls. Her daughter liked to give the dolls adult roles which gave Handler an idea. She approached her husband, Elliot, a co-founder of the Mattel toy company, with the idea for an adult doll for children. Handler ended up purchasing three German dolls called Bild Lilli that were just what she wanted—an adult-figured doll.

She reworked the doll back in the states, and the rest is history. Barbie made her debut on March 9, 1959, at the American International Toy Fair in New York, and this date became her birthday. Barbie's full name of Barbara Millicent Roberts came from a series of 1960's novels. Barbie lived in a fictional town called Willows, Wisconsin and attended Willows High School.

Time to Build - Amazing Facts About LEGO

We played with them as a kid, and now they're a great excuse to have kids, as long as you don't step on them in the middle of the night (the LEGOs, not the kids). They've been delighting (and frustrating) millions of people for decades, and they have an endless array of possibilities. Here's a look into to the amazing world of LEGO.

The LEGO name comes from the Danish phrase, "leg godt", which means, "play well".

The famous LEGO brick was patented on January 28, 1958, and all 2x4 bricks are produced to this standard today.

The amount of LEGO people produced is roughly 4 billion. That's more than the total of the top ten most populous countries with real humans.

There is an average of 86 LEGO pieces for every person on the planet.

The number of tires produced by LEGO makes it one of the world's largest tire manufacturers.

If you take just six 2x4 LEGO bricks to build with, they can be combined in 915,103,765 different combinations.

Each LEGO mini-figure is exactly four blocks tall.

In Budapest, Hungary, the world's tallest LEGO tower was constructed on May 25, 2014 from 450,000 bricks and rose to a height of 114 feet. It was topped with a Hungarian built Rubik's Cube.

James May of Surrey, Great Britain made the world's first full-size house made entirely out of LEGO bricks; 3.3 million bricks to be exact. The house took 1,200 volunteers over a month to build and was demolished shortly thereafter. The bricks were then donated to charity. The building of the house was done for May's television series, *James May's Toy Stories*. You may recognize May's name if you've ever seen the UK version (and original) *Top Gear*. He is one of the co-hosts of the program.

According to Warner Bros. Pictures, in order to make *The LEGO Movie* the creators used a total of 3,863,484 LEGO bricks mixed with computer animation. To make the entire film would have required 15,080,330 bricks, making the filming cost prohibitive.

How a Hedge Fund Repoed an Argentine Navy Ship

A U.S. hedge fund wanted their money back on debt they were owed by the country of Argentina. Here's the interesting way they went about making a point.

In 2001, Argentina defaulted on over $100 billion in debt. In the years that followed, the country discharged 93% of its debt, causing major losses for bondholders. The U.S. hedge fund, NML Capital, was part of the remaining 7% that hadn't been paid.

In 2012, NML Capital still owned over $1 billion of Argentine debt, but Argentina was unwilling to pay. NML Capital had been having trouble collecting, even with a U.S. court awarding them several billion dollars in damages, because Argentina's assets were protected by sovereign immunity laws.

An Argentine Navy ship, the *Libertad*, was sailing across the Atlantic in October of 2012, and this was when the hedge fund found their moment to strike in true repo-man fashion. They tracked the ship using the internet, and when the ship altered course from a planned stop in Nigeria due to worries over piracy, the ship docked in Ghana.

After the ship docked, NML Capital filed suit in a Ghana court and asked for an injunction to seize the ship. They argued that this was to partially fulfill payment on Argentina's debt. The judge in Ghana granted the request and ordered Argentina to pay $20 million to the court which would then go to NML Capital before the ship could be refueled to leave. Argentina refused.

The majority of the 326 person crew of the Libertad, which is a tall-mast sailing vessel used in training sailors of the Argentine navy, left the ship, leaving only the captain and a few other sailors with the ship.

The "standoff" lasted 10 weeks until an international tribunal for laws of the sea ordered Ghana to release the ship, agreeing with Argentina's claim that warships, under a U.N. convention, are immune from civil claims in foreign ports. The ship finally left the port and returned to Argentina.

The Argentine government called the hedge funds that owned their debt, "vulture funds", and continued to refuse to make any debt repayments to them. The battle continued and the U.S. Supreme Court got in on the action on June 16, 2014. They were going to decide if they would hear Argentina's appeal on the previous rulings that had ordered Argentina to pay back the billions of dollars they owed on their debt. Argentina was at risk of defaulting on their next debt payment of $13 billion that was to be due on June 30th if they lost their appeal to the Supreme Court or if the court decided not to review the case.

The Supreme not only declined to hear the appeal case, but also ruled in a 7-1 decision that bondholders could issue subpoenas to banks so they could trace Argentina's assets around the world. Argentina, in the mean time, has all but ignored the court's decision. This placed the country in contempt of court by U.S. District Judge Thomas Griesa. This one doesn't look like it will end anytime soon.

I Bet They Wish They Had a Do-Over

Google's founders were willing to sell to Excite for under $1 million in 1999, but Excite turned them down. What's Google's market value now? About $395 billion.

Excite was one of the internet's first portals, just as Google is today, and Excite CEO George Bell was the one who turned down the famous offer. Bell had a second chance when Google founders Larry Page and Sergey Brin were talked down to the price of $750,000. Bell turned them down again; mistake number two. There's no telling what Google would be like today if the sale had taken place, and they seem to be doing just fine on their own.

Excite on the other hand has not fared as well. In 2004, Excite was sold to Ask Jeeves, the one with the butler that helped you search things. This later became Ask.com. It's now owned by Barry Dillers IAC, a media and internet company. I'm sure those at Excite wished they had a do over.

Nothing is Certain In Life Except Death and Football?

Up until April 2015, the NFL never had to pay any taxes. It wasn't until mounting political pressure that the league finally decided to change their tax status after 70 years. Before this time and even though the NFL made approximately $10 billion a year, it was considered a non-profit and had a tax exempt status. It paid no federal taxes. As a side note, the NCAA, NHL, and PGA tour, continue to pay no federal taxes.

The NFL was considered a not-for-profit under the section 501 (c)(6) of the IRS code before their April 2015 decision. This is a specific section dealing with the status of boards of trade, chambers of commerce, and real estate boards not organized for profit. It says, straight from the code itself, "professional football leagues (whether or not administering a pension fund for football players)". This was even upheld in a court decision in 1983.

Now, the NFL itself didn't have to pay taxes, but the individual teams still had to. They control the salaries, ticket prices, and leases on stadiums, and are set-up as some particular type of corporation, thus they are for-profit businesses and have to pay taxes.

The sticky part of the situation arose because even though the NFL was there to be an entity representing the overall league, it did engage in business that brought in a profit, such as television deals. But the NFL didn't collect these profits from TV through the league office. It went, and continues to go, through another entity called NFL Ventures, a for-profit business that is owned by the 32 teams. The revenue from TV, sponsorships, and ticket sales is split among the teams. The NFL also wasn't required to disclose its financial numbers, so the only way to gauge its real earnings came from looking at the Green Bay Packers, a publicly traded company.

The NFL has a very complicated structure, and the one area that was hard for the NFL to explain to keep its tax-exempt status dealt with the amount it paid the NFL Commissioner, Roger Goodell. He made $44 million a year in 2012, and $35 million in 2013, which flew in the face of the area of the code that stated that a private shareholder or individual couldn't benefit from its net earnings as a non-profit.

While the move by the NFL won't result in a new, huge tax bill because of the way the organization is aligned, it does allow it to not to have to do something else. Because of the change in tax status, the NFL will no longer have to disclose what it pays Roger Goodell, or any of the other top executives of the NFL.

A Latte and a Piece of Stock, Please

The New York Stock Exchange started as a coffee shop. The Tontine Coffee House was established in 1793 on the northwest corner of Wall Street and Water Street. It was built as a place for stockbrokers to trade under the Buttonwood Agreement. This agreement meant that brokers at the coffee house would trade with each other only, and it became a center for all types of business dealings. The trading continued until 1817 when the New York Stock and Exchange Board (NYSEB) was created and a larger place was needed. The coffee house eventually became a tavern in 1826 and later a hotel in 1832. The NYSEB became the present-day New York Stock Exchange.

So That's What That Thing Is Called

The toothpaste blob you see on toothpaste packages and in advertisements is technically called a "nurdle". I couldn't find exactly why it is called a "nurdle", however, but I did find that it is also a cricket term meaning, "To score runs by gently nudging the ball in vacant areas of the field". It's also used to describe a cylindrical shaped plastic object used in the plastics or manufacturing industry. But the world of the "nurdle" is actually quite heated.

Colgate-Palmolive, the toothpaste maker, filed suit to prohibit the use of the nurdle in other companies' toothpaste packaging. It seemed to be a pre-emptive strike against GlaxoSmithKline, the maker of Aquafresh, and their application for a trademark for the nurdle on their packaging. Glaxo filed their own suit after Colgate had filed theirs. It's all rather confusing. Why can't everyone just use the nurdle and get along. It seems the war is only beginning. If you find it all too hard to fathom, just look it up if you don't believe me.

It's a Sports World After All

ESPN, which is owned by the Walt Disney Company, is responsible for over half of Disney's operating income, and makes more profit than all other Disney divisions combined. The Walt Disney

Company has movie studios, theme parks, products, a line of cruise ships, and owns the TV network ABC, but most of its profits come from ESPN as well as a contribution from the Disney Channel.

ESPN was acquired when Disney bought Capital Cities/ABC in 1996. ESPN was already expanding and the executives at Disney recognized the network's potential. ESPN generates $6.1 billion in affiliate fees for Disney, and ad revenues from the network are around $3.3 billion. ESPN is currently worth about $40 billion while Disney is worth about $84 billion. ABC on the other hand is worth a paltry $1.7 billion. Mickey has never been more proud he helped out with such a good deal.

So That's Where All That Oil Comes From

It's a common misconception that the United States imports most of its domestic oil from the Middle East, when in fact, the U.S. imports over half of its oil from North and South America with only 28% coming from the Middle East. Who is the largest importer to the U.S.? Canada, with 1.14 billion barrels of oil imported in 2013, more than double that of the next country. That amount is about 21.7 billion gallons of gasoline.

Between 1997 and 2010, the U.S. did import more oil than it produced, but that all began to change around 2005 when the trend began to reverse. Oil produced in the U.S. and used here now stands at around 60%, with 40% of the oil being imported.

A Hurricane Party

When Hurricane Frances moved toward the Florida coast in 2004, Wal-Mart employed one of its latest pieces of shopping tendency gadgetry, a data program it calls "predictive technology". Wal-Mart wanted to find out what shoppers were going to buy before the big storm hit.

They first looked at what happened when Hurricane Charley struck the coast in August of 2004. The storm had landed just weeks before. Based on the shopper's history from that time, Wal-Mart began to try and predict what shoppers would do this time before Hurricane Frances struck. They were able to pull from their data what the top selling items ahead of a hurricane would be, and what they discovered was rather interesting. The top seller was beer (no surprise there), and strawberry Pop-Tarts, which sold seven times greater than normal. They used this information to ship extras of these and other products to Wal-Marts in the storm's path.

Getting the data to figure this out isn't difficult for Wal-Mart. With about 100 million customers that grace the stores each week, the company sits on a treasure trove of information. Wal-Mart is said to have 460 terabytes of data on its databases in the corporate headquarters in Bentonville, Arkansas. That's enough data to double the amount of data on the Internet.

The company has paid a tidy sum for the technology, specifically a private system that tracks product sales called Retail Link, upwards to the tune of $1.4 billion dollars. So essentially your buying habits are being tracked anytime you check out from a store, but Wal-Mart keeps the information secret because they don't want the competition to know their next moves. Think about that when you buy that next bag of cheese puffs.

The Real Meaning of Yahoo

The website, "Yahoo", is an acronym for "Yet Another Hierarchical Officious Oracle." The made-up acronym came from Jerry Yang and David Filo in 1994 when they started a website collection called, "Jerry and David's Guide to the World Wide Web".

The entries were arranged in a hierarchy, while "oracle" was used since it sounded officious, which is defined as an annoying person who tries to tell others what to do in a way that isn't wanted or needed.

The term "yahoo" was first used in Jonathan Swift's 1726 novel, *Gulliver's Travels*, and described a crude, dirty brute of the land of the Houyhnhnms.

Being that Yang and Filo were college students at the time and were just wanting to be funny, they thought of themselves as the later definition of a "yahoo", which is an uncultivated, boorish, or uncouth person.

Hold On to Those Pennies

The reason the penny just doesn't make any sense anymore (pardon the pun) is that the U.S. penny costs over 2 cents to make, and nickels don't fare much better. For the year 2013, the U.S. taxpayers lost $105 million on the production of pennies and nickels.

Why the change? Minting costs increased because the cost of the metals used to make the coins went up. The nickel contains copper and nickel, and the penny contains copper and zinc. As the metal prices climbed during the early 2000s, the cost of minting increased. Since 2006 the penny and the nickel has lost the Treasury money due to the production of these coins.

THAT'S ENTERTAINMENT

I Wasn't Just Imagining Things

It's common that you will see the same six commercials during each ad break during TV showings of the movie, *Groundhog Day*, (in reference to what's happening to Bill Murray in the movie, if you didn't happen to make the connection). Another variation is to have an ad break with the same six commercials. This is a method of repeated advertising, but this particular version ramps it up a notch to imitate what happens to Bill Murray in the movie.

Other forms of repeated advertising are done so the ad will stick with the person watching it. Interestingly, there are quotas that a network or station must meet in how many times a commercial is shown in a month (apart from this example for Groundhog Day). They sometimes will have to play the same commercial many times near the end of the month to meet this quota. Watch for this example the next time you see the movie, and remember, "Don't drive angry!"

Order in the Court! How Real Are T.V. Judges?

Judge Wapner of *The People's Court* was the first to dispense justice from the bench on T.V. Many have followed in his footsteps; Judge Judy, Judge Mathis, Judge Joe Brown, etc. They seem to hand out justice, but looks can be deceiving.

Court T.V. shows are nothing but a set that looks like a court. Sorry to burst your bubble, but they're not a court at all. The judges put themselves in black robes, and in the case of Judge Judy, that little white doily. They were all real court judges in some capacity before their T.V. appearances, but they are merely wearing costumes at this point because these judges have no real judging power.

In the beginning of the show there is always a statement to the effect of, "The parties have agreed to have their disputes settled here." The participants must agree to dismiss their court cases (from small claims court) and submit the case to binding arbitration. That's what these "judges" are now, arbitrators (even though they had been a real judge in the past).

An arbitrator is an independent person officially appointed to settle a dispute. The parties sign a contract to agree to the arbitrator's decision, but here is the kicker in these court shows—the defendant never really loses, nor do they ever have to pay. The shows pay the participants an appearance fee, they fly them out to the filming, and put them up in a hotel.

Another funny aspect (and entirely true as I heard from someone on one of these shows) is that the show will pay for a person to get a new set of teeth, or complete dental work. No one wants to see bad teeth on their TV set. Before appearing, the litigants are coached on how they should prepare and act, even how they should dress.

The producers want good T.V. and not some boring affair, so the participants are revved up before the case. If the "judge" awards the decision to the plaintiff, the show pays them the reward. If the defendant prevails, then the plaintiff gets nothing. Both litigants get an appearance fee from the show. The defendant actually comes out ahead because they get an appearance fee and only have to defend their good name, if they have one.

Judge Judy makes $45 million a year being a fake judge, so not a bad gig. She never came close to that as a real judge. So the next time you see these shows, realize what you're watching is similar to attending an ad-libbed play.

Off to See the Wizard

We all love the musical *Wicked* (don't deny it) and the late 70s movie, *The Wiz*, but what the heck does "Oz" mean, and where did it come from? Frank Baum, the creator of the "Wizard of Oz", thought up the name "Oz" when he happened to look at his filing cabinet and saw the labels A-N, and O-Z of the alphabetic filing system; hence the name, "Oz." Thank goodness he didn't think "Anoz" sounded better.

That Really is All, Folks

Mel Blanc, the man of a thousand voices, and the man behind the voices of Bugs Bunny, Elmer Fudd, and Speedy Gonzales (just to name a few), immortalized one of his most famous lines on his epitaph in the Hollywood Memorial Cemetery. It reads: "That's All, Folks." Other well-known names in the cemetery are Cecil B. DeMille, Bugsy Siegel, and Rudolph Valentino.

Hollywood's Most Famous Scream

The Wilhelm scream is possibly the most famous piece of stock sound footage that has been played in a wide variety of movies. It has been used in over 200 films starting since 1951. It's a good bet you've heard it more than once.

The Wilhelm scream was believed to originate during the 1951 western, *Distant Drums*. One of the soldiers in the movie gets bitten and dragged underwater by an alligator, and the scream was recorded in a different take. The sound was likely voiced by actor Sheb Wooley. The sound is named after the character, Private Wilhelm, from the 1953 western, *The Charge at Feather River*. Wilhelm gets shot by an arrow and belts out the now famous sound effect.

Sound Designer, Ben Burtt, found the sound clip by chance many years later, appropriately titled, "Man being eaten by alligator". He then inserted the sound into a scene of *Star Wars*, and Burtt is credited with naming it the Wilhelm scream. Burtt continued to use the sound effect in movies he worked on, including all of the *Star Wars* and *Indiana Jones* movies. The sound became a sort of in-house joke between sound designers, and they began to spread the use of the clip.

Since 2011 the sound clip has been used in over 225 movies, video games, and TV shows. Peter Jackson, director of the *Lord of the Rings*, even used it in his productions.

It's a Wonderful Sesame Street?

Sesame Street's Bert and Ernie were named after Bert the cop and Ernie the taxi driver in Frank Capra's, *It's a Wonderful Life*. Now there is a caveat to this rather useless fact, it may or may not be 100% true. Some sources have said that it was merely coincidence and that the names were used because the writers liked them. But there are other reasons why it has persisted. In a 1996 special called *Elmo Saves Christmas*, Bert and Ernie walk by a TV set playing the movie and hear the dialogue from George Bailey played by Jimmy Stewart when he says, "Bert! Ernie! What's the matter with you two guys? You were here on my wedding night."

Another reason the fact or rumor has continued is because it has been reinforced by some credible sources. The rumor was on a 35th anniversary trivia quiz on Sesamestreet.org run by the Sesame workshop, it was confirmed by Gary Knell, the CEO of Sesame Workshop, and it appeared on the *Sesame Street Live* Facebook page. Without Jim Henson to ask, we'll never really know.

Elvis Has Left the Whitehouse

Elvis, the King of Rock and Roll, was one interesting cat, man. His life was scattered with numerous oddities and fascinating facts. One of the most amazing was his desire to meet with the President of the United States. The King had some important things to discuss.

To describe Elvis's life as "interesting" would be an understatement. He had a pet monkey named Scatter, he dyed his hair black from his natural blonde (to appear more edgy), his crew was known as the "Memphis Mafia" and had gold and diamond rings with the letters "TCB" scrolled on top (for "Taking Care of Business").

The King made 31 movies and 2 music documentaries and recorded over 600 songs, none of which he wrote, but he made 149 of these songs appear in the top 100, 114 in the top 40, 40 in the top 10, and 18 into number one hits. Despite a huge worldwide following, Elvis only performed 5 shows outside of the U.S., and all of those shows were in Canada. The only time he was in Great Britain was during a layover after a plane flight. And the list goes on, and on, and on.

Now we can go on to the drugs. They deserve a list all their own. There is no doubt Elvis was a pro at taking vast quantities of narcotics later in his career. Even an elephant couldn't compete. His personal physician testified that Elvis had been prescribed, by him, over 5,000 narcotic capsules and pills in the seven months before he died. Great doctor, right? The autopsy later revealed he had eight different barbiturates and narcotics at the time of his death, but the Chief Medical Examiner of Tennessee at the time signed that the cause of death was because of a coronary problem–hmmm…you think?

There is no doubt that Elvis is clearly a fascinating character, but the one factoid I seem to find the most interesting—and I don't know why—was about the famous meeting between Richard Nixon and Elvis. Elvis penned a letter on American Airlines stationary while up in the air about meeting with the president to discuss drug abuse by the youth of America. He wanted to clean things up. The ironic thing was, Elvis wrote the letter while on drugs.

Elvis got his meeting with the president—after giving up his personal Colt .45 pistol to the Secret Service. He then convinced the President to name him as a Federal Agent at Large in the fight against drugs, and after a little convincing, Elvis got his badge from Nixon.

It was later reported that Elvis used his new badge to assist motorists after accidents or to pull them over for speeding. I'm not sure if he did it in his velvet suit, however. It was more than a year later that the Washington Post broke the story about the clandestine meeting.

The oddities in Elvis' life many times overshadow his charity, but even after his death in 1977, Elvis continues to pack 'em in. Graceland receives over 600,000 visitors a year, and there are over 400 Official Elvis fan clubs in the world. Way to go King.

A Really Good Lunch Meeting

Pixar head John Lasseter and his team came up with the ideas for *A Bug's Life*, *Finding Nemo*, *Monsters, Inc.*, and *WALL-E* at a single lunch meeting in 1994. It was a year before the Pixar release of *Toy Story* and Andrew Stanton, Pete Docter, Joe Ranft, and current Pixar head, John Lasseter, met at a place called Hidden City Cafe near the Pixar studios. As of 2012, the place had been closed, but that didn't stop the animators from paying homage to the spot where they came up with these great ideas. A reference to the place is seen on a license plate in *Toy Story 2*, and a shop front in *Monsters, Inc.* Now that's being efficient and using your time wisely.

No Acceptance Speech From These Stars

There are fifteen fictional characters that have stars on Hollywood's 'Walk of Fame'. The List includes: Big Bird, Bugs Bunny, Donald Duck, Godzilla, Kermit the Frog, Mickey Mouse, The Munchkins, The Muppets, The Rugrats, Shrek, The Simpsons, Snow White, Tinker Bell, Winnie the Pooh, and Woody Woodpecker. In addition to these characters, there are three animal stars on the Walk of Fame: Lassie, Rin Tin Tin, and Strongheart. Daffy Duck is still upset on not being included.

This Bet Was Set, He Did Not Fret

Dr. Suess had a bet with his publisher, Bennett Cerf, that he couldn't complete a book with only 50 words. Dr. Seuss won when he wrote "Green Eggs and Ham". Theodore Seuss Geisel published it in 1960. The 50 words in Green Eggs in Ham, in alphabetically order are: a, am, and, anywhere, are, be, boat, box, car, could, dark, do, eat, eggs, fox, goat, good, green, ham, here, house, I, if, in, let, like, may, me, mouse, not, on, or, rain, Sam, say, see, so, thank, that, the, them, there, they, train, tree, try, will, with, would, you. The bet was for $50.

More Than a Challenging Acting Job

The *African Queen* was an adventure film from 1951 that was directed by John Huston that starred Humphrey Bogart and Katherine Hepburn. It was, to say the least, a tough set. The crew fought off bugs, heat, and a host of other things to get the movie made. The entire cast and crew even came down with dysentery, except for the director, Huston, and actor, Bogart. They chose to drink whisky instead of water and lived off only canned food. The water had been the source of the problem. Bogart later said, "All I ate was baked beans, canned asparagus and Scotch whisky."

A Sitting Spud

The term "couch potato" has nothing to do with the laziness of the potato, which seem to work very hard anyway, but came about from a wise crack. Cartoonist Robert Armstrong liked to watch television, and his friends knew it. In July 1976, one of Armstrong's friends, named Tom Iacino, called him on the phone. Armstrong's girlfriend answered, and Iacino, sensing where Armstrong was since he didn't answer the phone, asked, "Hey, is the couch potato there?" Armstrong found the phrase so funny that he later published a cartoon of a potato sitting on a couch.

Armstrong and Iacino were members of an intentionally humorous group called the "Boob Tubers" which was created in 1973 to respond to California's growing health-craze around that time. The main goal of the "Boob Tubers" was to sit around and watch TV while eating junk food. Now the term, couch potato, really gave their group traction. In 1979, they called themselves the Couch Potatoes and put a float in the Doo Dah Parade which parodied the Tournament of Roses Parade. This prompted the first written use of the word which appeared in a 1979 LA Times article covering the event.

Armstrong went on to produce many pieces of merchandise with the phrase and even trademarked it in 1979, but it was already becoming too popular. Despite Armstrong's efforts to keep it as a legitimate trademarked term, he was unsuccessful, and media outlets began to use it, as did most everyone else, to describe a person who just sits around and watches TV.

THE NARROW WORLD OF SPORTS

Winter Olympic Events–Gone, But Not Forgotten

One can't help but wonder about the many athletes who can't compete in the Winter Olympics since their event is no longer offered in the games. Here we will pay homage to those sports that once had their moment in the sun (or snow).

Men's Special Figures – This event made its one appearance at the Summer Games of 1908 in London. There were no Winter Games at that time. It involved skaters making intricate designs in the ice. And here's an interesting side note. Ever wonder why figure skating is called figure skating? No? Well, too bad, I'm going to tell you anyway. Skaters had to make figure eights as a part of the competition. These skaters had to compete in a figure event prior to making all those leaps, jumps, and spins. It was eventually eliminated in the 1990s.

Skijouring – This event was pretty simple; grab a horse or a dog by the reins and have it pull you on your skis. It made its Olympic debut as a demonstration sport at the 1928 Winter Olympics in St. Moritz, Switzerland. It continues to be a sport today, just not in the Olympics.

Ice Stock Sport – Also called Bavarian curling, this sport is of German origin. The Olympic organizers must have felt that curling by itself was enough to hold everyone's interest. Competitors slide a block by using a stick attached to the top of it. They either try to hit a target, or see how far they can slide it. Ice stock was a demonstration sport in 1936 and somehow made a comeback in 1964.

Bandy – This sport has been described as a cross between soccer and hockey. There are eleven players per side, and they play on a rink the size of a soccer field. This sport uses sticks similar to hockey sticks and a small ball. It made its debut and exit at the 1952 Winter Olympics in Oslo, Norway. This sport continues to this day. The U.S. even has a National Bandy Team.

Speed Skiing – This sport is for all the adrenaline junkies out there and you have to have nerves of steel to compete. The most characteristic aspect of speed skiing is the outfits. Skiers have latex suits with giant turtle-like helmets that offer maximum aerodynamics. Speeds reach over 100 mph and the world record is a blistering 156 mph. The skiers simply race downhill in a straight line, and whoever has the fastest time wins.

Speed skiing was a demonstration sport in the 1992 Winter Olympics in Albertville, France. Unfortunately, the speeds and danger never allowed this sport to continue in the games because of the death of skier after they crashed into a grooming machine during warm-ups. The sport continues to this day, but the speeds are limited to 124 mph by the International Ski Federation.

Synchronized skating – This particular event has to be seen to be believed, and was a demonstration sport as recent as 2002. Eight to twenty skaters perform on the ice at one time, and you guessed it, they're synchronized.

Snowshoeing – This event was also an exhibition at the 2002 Olympics. It's pretty simple—slap on some high-tech snowshoes and run like the wind.

Ski Ballet – This event involves a skier gracefully executing turns, jumps, rolls, and spins while skiing down the slopes to music. It made a demonstration appearance in the 1988 Games in Calgary, and in 1992 at the Games in Albertville, France. I'm not sure why, but there is something disconcerting about ski ballet when you see it performed.

Military Patrol – This particular sport made its appearance in 1924 in Chamonix, France, and later was a demonstration sport in the 1928, 1936, and 1948 Olympics. It involved three things; cross country skiing, shooting, and mountaineering, and its participants were actual military units. Happily, it later evolved into the modern biathlon, without the military part of course.

Many of these events continue to take place today without being in the Olympics, but don't be surprised if you see one or two of them crop up again at the next Winter Games.

5 Unusual Sports to Watch During Any Season

There comes a time when you just need something a little different—very different. Here are five sports you can check out to protect yourself from common sports overload.

Sepak Takraw – A sport popular in Asia, Sepak Takraw is a cross between badminton, volleyball, and soccer that uses kicks to send a ball made of dried palm leaves over a net. I'm sure there are a lot of pulled hamstrings in this one. What better reason to watch.

Chess Boxing – The name says it all. Try to beat your opponents face in, then sit down for a friendly chess match. Repeat this process until; 1) you or your opponent get knocked out, or 2) win the chess match. If neither of those can be accomplished then the refs will decide your fate (not sure if they take into account the player's chess skills in the decision).

Cricket – The game of Cricket is not that bizarre to millions of people around the world, but for Americans, it's like trying to understand Form 8824 from the IRS. Terms such as bails, wickets, all-rounder, wicketkeeper, crease, and sixer can confuse even the most devoted sportsmen. Instead of me trying to explain the rules, find a handy guide, and you too can spend your spring, summer, and possibly the fall trying to understand this incredibly difficult game.

Buzkashi – This is a traditional game played in Central Asia. It can be described as a form of polo, since the teams of ten ride horses, but that is where the similarities end. Unlike polo, where the players hit a ball with a mallet, these players drag a very dead goat or cow toward the opposition's goal line. I doubt this will be a "sport" you'll see on ESPN anytime soon.

Wife Carrying – What could be more fun than carrying your wife around on your back? Why doing it to win a prize of course. While wife carrying even has a North American Championship, its origins are Finnish, where it is known as Eukonkanto. If you get good at carrying your wife at the World Championships you can win her weight in beer. That could be quite a score if your wife was of the, uh, larger variety. If this has piqued your interest and you would like to carry your wife, just contact your local wife carrying organization.

Now I'm not sure where you would catch these on the sports channels—maybe ESPN 24. It may take some effort, but expand your horizons and pick a new sport to follow. The question is, are you going to watch?

How Much Playing Really Goes On in an NFL Football Game?

The big Sunday game is on and you've settled in to your comfy recliner for the afternoon battle between two league favorites. With a chicken wing in one hand and a beer in the other you prepare for the endless action on the gridiron.

But there is something going on here. Something that you probably don't realize in amongst the endless commentaries, replays, reviews, commercials, and stats. This game may appear long and full of action, but in reality, it adds up to the length of half a sit-com minus the commercials. This is the true length of an NFL game.

There is a secret hidden during NFL games. We may not realize it, but there is very little football that is actually played. Yes, the players run around, return to the huddle and repeat, but the time that the players actual play the game is astoundingly small. Eleven minutes. Yup, in a 3-hour game the time the ball is in play equals about eleven minutes.

It's not anyone's fault, that's just the way the game is played. I'm sure if you examined baseball (which should be taken into consideration) the time the ball is in play is probably even less. That's not the case, however. Baseball play time runs a little over 17 minutes for a 3-hour game. But we're talking about football.

How are 3-hours of time with only eleven minutes of actual play still riveting on TV? It's a feat of television engineering. Commercials take up most of it, and everyone needs to take a bathroom break and have time to grab their favorite beverage. There is a little over an hour of commercials in a typical broadcast. What else goes on? The players do a lot of running and standing without doing anything with the ball. About an hour of this goes on during a typical game. There will be three minutes of reviews and about seventeen minutes of replays that relive the, on average, four second play. Since replays can be put in slow-motion, this helps to increase their time on-screen.

There are approximately 133 plays in an NFL game, but this number varies on the state of the game. An exciting end of half or end of game where a team is driving the field without doing the "run out the clock" scenario influences this number. The cheerleaders get a lot of face time, right? Actually, no. They get a disappointing average of 3 seconds on the screen. Darn.

The time in an NFL telecast is filled with countless other things to stretch out the broadcast—human interest stories, views of the stadium, players on the sideline, fans in the stands, views of the commentators, stats, halftime, etc, etc. The networks have become wizards at gluing us to our TVs and filling 2 hours and 49 minutes of time with no actual football action, spending $150,000 to $250,000 per telecast.

Now what if you don't have the time to watch all your favorite games? It's possible to do so, if you had a way to break every game down to just when the football was in action. To watch every NFL in a given week, you would only need to devote 2.9 hours, about the time of one typical, full NFL game. That's sixteen games in under three hours; all the action without any of the distractions. To watch the entire regular NFL season, all 208 games, you would need to be a little more devoted and spend a total of 38 hours. It could be done in a month. For that same time you could opt to watch one full game, every week for the entire regular season. That would be thirteen games. If you're super hardcore about your NFL football, and wanted to see every game of the regular season in their entirety, then you would need to set aside 603 hours, or 25 days. I hope you have some sick time you can use from work.

But the point of football, and probably what makes it so popular on TV, is the drama, the endless commentary about each play, and how the flow of the game changes in a heartbeat. The replays don't hurt either. So you have a choice, record the game on your DVR and watch only the plays, saving yourself two hours and forty-nine minutes of your life. Or grab another chicken wing and settle in to watch the pageantry and the show, even if it might mean you only get to see that one game for the week.

The First Unlikely Marathon Winner

Spiridon Louis, a Greek shepherd, won the first modern marathon at the 1896 Athens Olympics. The marathon originated because of the legend of Pheidippides. It was said that in 490 B.C., after running the distance from Marathon to Athens with news the Greek had defeated the Persians at the Battle of Marathon, Pheidippides collapsed and died. The first marathon commemorated this event and had a field of 25 men ready to compete at the 1896 Olympic Games.

Louis was not a runner or an athlete, his job was to transport fresh water to Athens. He qualified for the event by finishing a preliminary race in which he placed fifth. Louis took the lead in the Olympic marathon after about 20 miles. He got so far ahead that he even stopped during the race to have a glass of cognac (or wine as some say) at an inn before continuing. He finished in 2 hours, 58 minutes, and 50 seconds. The 2014 New York Marathon, just to put things into perspective, was finished by the fastest runner in a time of 2 hours, 10 minutes, and 59 seconds. Not bad for a guy that never trained to run the marathon. Spiridon Louis never ran another race after that one, but why would he have needed to?

Why A Treadmill Feels Like Prison

We've all spent countless hours on that incessant machine, whiling away our time and spending most of it watching the seconds tick past tirelessly slow. But where did the term treadmill come from and why do we sometimes want to smash it with a rock? Well, there's a valid reason why a treadmill feels like a medieval torture device.

The first treadmills were used by our four legged friends of the larger variety, the horse. A horse treadmill was patented in the early 1800s to do work, albeit not too well, but soon our smaller four-legged friend, the dog, was pressed into action. The dog was introduced to a home version of the treadmill and completed such menial tasks as churning butter. But the term treadmill still had not been coined. It was the humans and their two leg's time to get in on the action.

So where in the world did the term treadmill come into play? The answer dates back to the early 1800s when Sir William Cubitt, an English engineer, decided this would be a novel way to rehabilitate prisoners. It was collectively known as a tread wheel and looked like a giant hamster wheel. Prisoners would step on something that closely resembling a paddle wheel and away they would go, rehabbing themselves to their heart's content and sometimes upwards of ten hours a day. This would equate with climbing the equivalent of a small mountain, or around 8,000 vertical feet, as punishment. Someone finally got the bright idea this technique could be used more efficiently and the prisoners began to use the contraption to grind grain in a mill, hence the term treadmill. This practice went on until the late 1800s when finally it was deemed too cruel a punishment.

It wasn't until the 1950s when Dr. Robert Bruce established it as an important piece of medical testing equipment for cardiac patients, hence the cardiac stress test. The Bruce Protocol is still in use today during cardiac stress testing to diagnose certain heart conditions. The mainstream population was still without the wonders of the treadmill, and it wasn't until the late 1960's when Dr. Kenneth Cooper (of the Cooper Institute in Dallas, Texas, and in existence to this day) brought the treadmill to the masses with his research on the benefits of aerobic exercise.

So now when you're puffing away those pounds on the endless belt that never stops, just remember, it could be worse.

Get On Your Running Shoes

The New York Marathon is the largest marathon in the world. In 1970, 127 runners ran the NY Marathon, and in 2013, 50,304 did.

The initial course ran around Central Park only. Now the course meanders through all five boroughs of New York City. 2.5 million spectators watch the race, and a prize of $130,000 goes to the first place male and female runners. The marathon has only been cancelled once, in 2012, due to the damage left by Hurricane Sandy a week before the race was scheduled to be run.

Finally, Debt Free

It took thirty years, but Canadian citizens finally finished paying for the 1976 Montreal Summer Olympic Games. The final payment was made in November 2006. The cost of the games was expected to be $300 million, but the final bill was nearly $2 billion. Mismanagement and cost overruns were blamed for the ballooning cost of the games.

Because of the problems Montreal had with the Summer Olympics, many cities were scared off to host the games in 1984. Los Angeles was able to bid for those games without competition and dictated the terms of the deal to the International Olympic Committee. Instead of new facilities, Los Angeles used existing ones, and they relied on private financing. The result? The Los Angeles 1984 Summer Olympic Games came through with a tidy profit, something I'm sure the people of Montreal wished they had done. But they shouldn't worry since they're not alone. The 2004 Summer Olympics in Athens was considered a financial disaster as Greece went over budget by 60% and built too many hotel rooms. They thought the Olympics would lead to a large rise in tourism.

DIVE INTO THE WORLD OF TECHNOLOGY

So That's What It Means

Google got its name from the word "googol", which refers to the number one with a hundred zeros after it. It meant to represent the company's mission to organize the web's limitless amount of information. The word Google in the dictionary now means "to search for information on the Internet using the search engine Google".

A Scary and Cool Spy Trick You've Probably Never Heard Of

What if someone just around the corner could see what you're looking at on your computer screen without a physical or wireless connection and without ever even being in your system? Sounds like fiction, and it sounds scary. But it's based in reality, and it's been around for a long time.

Not to fear (I think), because the NSA has been on the case. The process I'm talking about is called Van Eck phreaking. Ever heard of it? Not many people have. Van Eck phreaking is the detection of electromagnetic emissions to spy on what is displayed on a CRT (cathode ray tube) or LCD (liquid-crystal display) monitor as well as the inputs coming from a computer keyboard. In 1995, Wilm van Eck published a paper and the first proof of concept on the idea. He even explained that it could be done from a large distance.

What makes Van Eck phreaking so scary is that it is untraceable. Intrusions are usually done through a computer network, making detection or the ability to trace the action possible. With Van Eck phreaking that is impossible.

The electromagnetic radiation that is emitted from a computer monitor and the cord linking the monitor, or even the keyboard and its cord, can be picked up by an antenna array and displayed on another monitor. All of the information that is on the screen will be displayed as the user sees it, and no one would even know its happening.

The NSA has a codename for this type of spying called TEMPEST. TEMPEST includes information and methods on how to spy on others as well as countermeasures to protect a computer system against this spying. The NSA's methods are of course classified on how to do this type of spying, but the standards for protecting oneself against this spying are well known and have been released. Not only does TEMPEST address spying dealing with electromagnetic radiation, but it also addresses spying through mechanical vibrations or sounds.

Even though this sounds terrible that someone could be spying on you looking at that fuzzy, cute cat picture, I would bet it's not something to worry about. But corporations and government entities have a real threat from this type of intrusion. Many companies, as well as the government, take this threat seriously and have countermeasures in place. One way they counter a possible attempt is by shielding electromagnetic emission with other metals, or encasing a room with metal walls. Another countermeasure involves scrambling the video signal so that the signal is much harder to be reproduced. See? There really isn't anything to worry about.

But hold on. Research completed in 2004 about the risk of eavesdropping on the electromagnetic signals from flat-panel displays and laptops found that they were susceptible and the ability to spy on them could be done with equipment that cost less than $2000. Let's hope this doesn't catch on.

A Computer and Water Sometimes Do Mix

In 1936, a Russian scientist, Vladimir Lukyanov, made a computer that ran on water. The computer was the first for solving partial differential equations. Lukyanov used water-filled tubes that were interconnected, and plugs changed the variables in the equation. The water level in specific tubes gave the answer to the problem.

A later example of this same type of computer using fluid was made in 1949 by Bill Phillips, a New Zealand economist. It was called the MONIAC, or Monetary National Income Analogue Computer, and also known as the Phillips Hydraulic Computer. Similar to the Russian computer, the MONIAC used fluid to solve a problem, in this case the workings of the economy of the United Kingdom. It used a large tank of fluid as the treasury and used colored water to represent the flow of money around the economy. Taps were used to flow water from the treasury to tanks that represented segments of the economy, and a pump was used to resupply the treasury tank to represent taxation. And you thought water was only for drinking.

Who Really Invented the Internet?

We have all heard the comment before that Al Gore said he invented the internet, but no, he did not, and no, he really never said he had. The statement was rather clumsily worded, but he never actually said he had "invented" it. It stemmed from a CNN interview in 1999, in which he said that he, "took the initiative in creating the internet," when he was asked what made him different than his challenger, Bill Bradley, for the Democratic presidential nomination. So if he didn't invent it, then who did?

The beginnings of the internet really can't be traced to just one person, but to a series of events that made it possible to exist. It started with President Dwight D. Eisenhower's creation of the Advanced Research Projects Agency, or ARPA, in 1958. The creation of the agency was in direct response to the Soviets' launching of Sputnik, the first man-made satellite in space. Its purpose was to expand the reach of technology and science beyond the current requirements of the military. It was also created to prevent a moment of surprise again in the areas of technological advancement.

Computers during this time in the 50s used punch cards, magnetic tape, and were enormous in size. There was also no way for computers to be networked together. No computer had access to another computer's data, and since the computers during this time had poor processing power, this posed a serious problem for a computer's capability, as well as its ability to decentralize information.

In 1969, a breakthrough was made in this area. ARPA enlisted the help of a company called Bolt, Beranek and Newman (BBN), to implement the world's first network, called ARPANET. ARPANET was initially connected by four Interface Message Processors (IMP). The IMPs were gateways, or what would later be called routers to you and me today. I'm no computer scientist, but for simplicities sake, we won't get into how they operated. Just knowing they acted like a router should be enough. You just have to remember that starting a network in the 60s was in no way like it is today.

There were four of these IMPs in the ARPANET: One at UCLA, one at Stanford, one at UC Santa Barbara, and one at the University of Utah. Each place employed a different computer of the time period (and different methods of operation). It's amazing they ever even got it to work.

On October 29, 1969, the first ever computer-to-computer link was made. A programmer at UCLA sent a message to Stanford, and the message was supposed to read "login", but the "L" and "O" were the only letters transmitted before the entire system crashed. They managed to get things working again and were then successful in sending the entire message the second time around. The birth of the internet had begun.

The first permanent link was established about a month later, and in December of '69 the four-node network was connected together. These connections established the protocols on how the internet runs today.

By the time the 1970s rolled around, researchers had figured out a way to connect ARPANET to the packet radio network, or PRNET. The PRNET was a way to connect computers with radio or wireless communication links. In 1973 the two different networks were connected. In 1977, a third network, the satellite network (SATNET), was connected, which also connected the U.S. to Europe. These connections to one another were called inter-networking. This is how it came to be called the Internet. The Internet was now a small child.

The next great leap in the Internet's growth came about in the 1990s. Tim Berners-Lee came up with a way to more simply navigate the Internet. This is what became the World Wide Web, and Berners-Lee had invented it. The internet was now growing into a feisty teenager. But this is where confusion takes hold for some people. The Internet and World Wide Web are two distinctly different things. The Internet is a connection of networks while the World Wide Web is a way to navigate through and between these networks. Now you can correct anyone who incorrectly uses the term. The "http", or hypertext transfer protocol, is one of the navigation tools that Berners-Lee invented to allow us to find our way through the vast Internet.

So it's clear that no one person invented the internet, but instead it was a collective of people piggybacking on each other's accomplishments that ultimately led to its existence. If there is anyone to thank, it might just be the Russians back in 1957 when they launched Sputnik. If it weren't for that event, we may have never had the Internet. Happy surfing.

A New Type of Internet Connection

Facebook, the social network, announced in July 2015 that it had completed a project called Aquila which is a full-scale aircraft that will deliver wireless internet with lasers. Aquila has the wingspan of a Boeing 737, weighs less than a car, and is solar powered.

The drone aircraft will cruise between 60,000 and 90,000 feet and will be able to deliver data speeds at 10 gigabits per second. In addition, Facebook says that it will be able to connect a point the size of a dime at a ten mile range, and the aircraft will cruise for three months at a time.

The name Aquila is named after the constellation which is from Greco-Roman mythology and was a bird that carried Zeus's thunderbolts to battle. Goggle has its own project of the same sort, called Project Loon, which will use balloons instead of an aircraft. It all sounds great, but will I have to friend them to get it?

Just Climbed Mount Everest, Time to Send a Tweet

As of 2010, climbers going up Mt. Everest were able to surf the web, check emails, and make phone calls. A Nepalese telecom company installed eight 3G base stations along the route to the Everest base camp so tourists and climbers can receive weather reports or stay in touch with trip organizers and family. The highest station is at 17,000 feet and near the base camp.

The mobile coverage can reach the summit of Mount Everest, and several climbers have been able to make phone calls on top of the world. One British mountaineer made the first live video call in 2013 at the peak using his smartphone for an interview with the BBC but got into hot water with the Nepali government since he hadn't received prior approval to do so. Over 3,000 people have climbed to the summit since 1953 when Sir Edmund Hilary became the first to do so.

Information Overload

A lot can go on in one minute on the internet. Take a look at what happens in just 60 seconds.

204 million emails are sent
48,000 apps are downloaded by Apple users
277,000 tweets are sent on Twitter
2.4 million pieces of content are shared on Facebook
4 million search queries are done on Google
72 hours of new video is uploaded to YouTube
26,389 Reviews are put on Yelp
216,000 new photos are posted on Instagram
and, $83,000 is made by Amazon in sales.

Spam Is Horrible

Unsolicited and unwanted bulk emails, commonly known as "spam", have been around since the infancy of the internet. The term is thought to have originated from a sketch from Monty Python's Flying Circus. In the sketch, a restaurant menu's items all become SPAM, the meat product. The word is repeated over and over until a group of Vikings (remember this is Monty Python we're talking about) begin to sing and repeat the SPAM phrase until they are told to stop.

So it is generally, and loosely, accepted that the term for unwanted emails, and a general drowning out of real conversation, originated in chat rooms referring to this particular sketch. The first true documented case of spam occurred on March 31, 1993, when a Usenet user named Richard Depew accidentally posted 200 messages that were the same to a news related newsgroup. He apologized and called his accident spam.

While there are other origin stories for spam, it's clear that it is a nuisance and a problem. Over 70% of email messages sent are spam and many of them are attempting to steal a user's identity in some way, which is also known as phishing.

When You Just Have Time to Waste

Google search is known for having some interesting things happen when you type in the words on a search. Many of them are now gone (bye Pac-man), but some still exist. When you search for the word "tilt" or "askew" on Google, the search results come up tilted slightly to the right. Type in "do a barrel roll" or "Z or R twice" and the page will spin like you're in a fighter jet. If you put in "define anagram", witty Google comes back with, "nerd fame again" in the "Did you mean" area. This of course is an anagram of "define anagram". Typing in "Google in 1998", gives the site a retro, throwback feel to the great days of 1998, and when you type in "zerg rush", watch as 'O's descend on your search results and begin to gobble them up. You can fight them off with three clicks on each 'O', but they keep coming back for more. I'm glad the Google programmers have a sense of humor.

The First Growing Days of the Internet

In June 1993, there were 130 websites and only 1.5% of them were of the .com variety. By the end of the year, the number of websites had more than quadrupled to 623 websites with 4.6% being .com. In two more years the number of websites hit 100,000 and the .com sites were at 50%. Eighteen years later, in September of 2014, the number of websites hit one billion, and the percentage of .com registered domains is still just around 50%.

A SHORT BREAK FOR POLITICS AND GOVERNMENT

But Can a Justice Dunk?

The Supreme Court is known as the nation's highest court, but there's a court that's even higher. A basketball court that is. On the fifth floor of the United States Supreme Court building is a basketball court, three floors above the courtroom of the United States Supreme Court. It's aptly known as the "Highest Court in the Land". The room once housed journals, but in the 1940s it was made into a workout room. An installation of wooden backboards followed years later. No one is allowed to play while the real court is in session, and if someone happens to forget, a clerk from the court is sent up to remind them. So that means you can be reprimanded on the "highest court" while the highest court is in session. Confused yet?

Space Case

Everyone should be allowed to vote in an election no matter where they are, and that goes for space too. Texas is the only U.S. State that allows a resident to cast an absentee ballot from space. In 1997, the Texas legislature passed a bill so the astronauts that lived in the Houston area and trained at NASA's Johnson Space Center wouldn't miss out on their right to vote if they were orbiting the earth.

What "We the People" Pay Congress

Do you know how much your Congressman or woman makes doing a job that has a current approval rating of 6% who think they're doing a good or excellent job, and 65% rate their performance as poor, according to a Rasmussen poll at the time of this writing (not that any other time would matter)? The answer may or may not surprise you.

Why is Congress so "bad"? Are they not satisfied with their accommodations? Do they not like what is served in the cafeteria? It would take an abundance of research to really explain why the average American can't stand the job they're doing, but maybe it's just the pay. Maybe the taxpayer needs to fork over a few more bucks to get them on the right track. No, just kidding. I thought you would need a laugh. The one thing you shouldn't hear them complain about (but some have) is their pay.

Its public knowledge what a member of Congress makes, but maybe you haven't seen the numbers in a while. According to a report on January 7, 2014 by the Congressional Research Service on Congressional Salaries and Allowances, the last pay adjustment for Congress was in January of 2009. The salaries for Congress have not changed since then. But don't pull out your tissues just yet—Senators and Representatives still make $174,000 per year. The Speaker of the House pulls in $223,500, and the President pro tempore of the Senate, minority and majority leaders of the House, and minority and majority leaders of the Senate make $193,400. In addition, they are allowed 15% of their basic pay to be earned outside of their Congressional pay. This income cannot come from certain areas however, such as employment from a firm, corporation, or association.

Congress is also appropriated money for personnel, office expenses, and mail allowances (as if we use that so much now). Representatives have something called Members' Representational Allowance (MRA). It is used for travel, staff, office space, and supplies. The MRA has decreased in recent years due to certain House resolutions, and the average allowance is now $1.24 million. The personnel allowance of this amount is $944,671. This is the amount each Representative can use to employ up to 18 people with the option of four more if they fall under a specific category (part-time, paid intern, temps, etc). The remainder is used for office expenses and mail. The overall budget for the House for MRAs' is now at $573.9 million, which is actually down from the $660.0 million in 2010. Too bad the Great Recession started in early 2008.

At the other end of the Capitol, the Senators' Official Personnel and Office Expense Account (SOPOEA), is the Senators' office and personnel expense fund. The average for this account in the Senate is $3.2 million. The overall budget for this expense is $396.2 million in

2012, down from $422.0 million in 2010. This covers exactly what the account says—personnel and office expenses.

Along with the SOPOEA, Senators have an interesting perk with office space. They can have office space in a federal building in the state they represent. The office can be up to 5,000 square feet if the state's population is less than 3 million, and up to 8,200 square feet in a state with a population of over 17 million. In addition, they can have as many offices as they want; there is no restriction. Senators also get $40,000 to furnish their state offices up to 5,000 square feet.

Is your head swirling yet? It should be. But wait, there's more. Let's take a look at a few non-elected positions and what they get paid. In the House: Chief Administrative Officer, Clerk of the House, Sergeant at Arms, Chaplain, Legislative Counsel, Law Revision Counsel, Parliamentarian, Inspector General, Interparliamentary Affairs Director, and General Counsel to the House—$172,500. In the Senate: Secretary of the Senate, Sergeant at Arms and Doorkeeper, Legislative Counsel, Legal Counsel—$172,500. The Parliamentarian makes $171,315, and Chaplains make $155,500. I'm not sure why the House Chaplain gets paid more. I guess they're more rowdy over there.

So after all that is said and done, what do you think? Do we pay our Congress too much, or too little? I don't think they do a poor job because of the pay. But what if they're just struggling to make ends meet like the rest of us. That's enough stress to show up in poor job performance. Oh, I forgot to tell you one last tidbit of information. The average net worth for members of Congress? $1.01 million (House - $900,000 Senate - $2.79 million). Strike out there.

Obviously money is not why Congress is so "bad", but remembering how much we pay them helps when we want to complain. Shouldn't we expect better performance in everything a Congress member does, and shouldn't they be held to a higher standard? You bet. We pay them a lot of money so we should always expect the best. But who is ultimately to blame for their poor performance? Unfortunately, we are. We're the ones who elected them to office.

20 of the Best Pieces of Political Slang

The political jungle that is Washington D.C. is akin to lathering yourself in turkey leftovers and leaping into an alligator pit. And to navigate this underbelly of mouth breathers takes wits, gumption, and knowledge of the jargon and slang that is used to survive that great arena of democracy. Now that I've gotten that off my chest, here are 20 of the best pieces of slang to help you understand what they're saying in and around Capitol Hill.

Beltway – AKA, "Inside the Beltway". It refers to anything on the inside of Interstate 495 that circles Washington D.C. and anything of interest to those working and living in that area; namely politicians, lobbyists, and federal contractors. It was first thought to be used in the New York Times in 1975. And no, it's not what holds up the pants of a bulbous congressman.

Bimbo Factor – This tidbit involves a sex-scandal involving a male politician and the effect a person of the female persuasion has on them. Also known as the bimbo syndrome (there is no cure).

Bloviate – This one is near and dear to a politician's heart. It means to go on and on and on, usually in some type of pompous way. Now that sounds like pretty much all of them, doesn't it?

Christmas Tree – A bill that attracts many unrelated floor amendments. It's usually a minor bill where everyone piles on their piece of legislation. It's not known when it started, but in 1956, Time Magazine had an article called "The Christmas Tree Bill" that told about a farm bill that had over 100 amendments attached to it.

Echo Chamber – In politics, ideas and beliefs are reinforced and amplified in a repetitive way inside some type of enclosed system. Things are repeated and repeated once more and other ideas or opposing views are simply ignored or disallowed. To put it simply, if something is repeated enough times to like-minded people then those people will believe it to be true.

Farley's Law – Voters will decide on a presidential candidate they are most likely to vote for by mid-October. It was named for James Farley, the Postmaster General under Franklin D. Roosevelt. It's not to be confused with Faraday's Law, the basic law of magnetism that predicts how a magnetic field will interact with an electrical circuit to produce an electromotive force. Now do you think a politician would understand that?

Foggy Bottom – One of the oldest Washington D.C. neighborhoods and home to the U.S. Department of State, George Washington University, and Watergate complex, as well as many other government offices. The Soggy Bottom Boys have no connection to this place. Hint: from *O'Brother, Where Art Thou?*

Fudge Factory – A term coined by State Department Officer, John Franklin Campbell, as a synonym for the State Department from his book *The Foreign Affairs Fudge Factory*. I think you can figure out what he meant by the term.

Gucci Gulch – The area in Washington D.C. on K Street where many lobbyists base their headquarters. Enough said.

Iron Triangle – The term used to describe the relationship between congressional committees, the bureaucracy, and special interest groups when making policy decisions. I hear they hug a lot.

Jungle Primary – Also known as a nonpartisan blanket primary. This is a primary election when all candidates for the same office, regardless of party affiliation, run against each other. The candidates receiving the most votes and the second-most votes go on to the general election. It's like a really bad playoff system. It's almost like the College Football Playoff Committee.

Kool-Aid – More formally used as "drinking the Kool-Aid". It means that a person or group holds some unwavering belief without questioning it. It comes from the November 1978 Jonestown deaths where followers of Jim Jones committed suicide by drinking a cyanide laced powered drink. It was actually Flavor Aid, but Kool-Aid got stuck with it.

Lunch Lid – A reference to time when the president won't be making an appearance. Also known to reporters as the time when the White House won't release any important news while they're eating lunch. I thought reporters only feed at night.

Panda Hugger – An official or political activist who is very generous to or supports Communist China policies. A term that is actually racist toward pandas.

Peoria – "Will it play in Peoria?" A term to ask if something will play to Middle America, or "Main Street". It refers to the Illinois city of Peoria. Never been there, but I'm sure it's lovely.

Policy Wonk – An expert on policy that takes an obsessive interest in all minor details in policy and thus is known to be out of touch with things in the real world. There are multiple origins to the word "wonk". Two of the best that probably aren't true; it's the reverse spelling of the word "know", or it stands for WithOut Normal Knowledge.

Rump Session – A session that takes place at the end of the day, like the backside of an animal. That fits with politics.

Timber – This has been used as far back as 1854 and refers to the character required of a person to hold a particular political office, possibly describing the strength of a particular tree. Hold it...Politicians have character?

Turkey Farm – The term used for underperformers in a particular department of the federal government, or a political dumping ground where political positions can be easily filled by a political appointment. Not much more to add there.

Zoo Plane – The term for all the leftover reporters, TV crews, and technicians that aren't allowed in Air Force One or some other plane carrying the news story and have to fly on a separate plane. It was first used during the Nixon Administration when the press aide for Nixon didn't like what one of the reporters had wrote about the then candidate for president. He joked that the reporter, "would never get off the zoo plane after this."

There are about a million others that come out of D.C. One thing is for certain, there are a few other choice words we could use for things coming out of Washington.

No Matter How Hard They Look, They'll Never Figure It Out

NASA will be spending $3 million from December 2012 to December 2017 to try to understand one of the greatest mysteries to mankind (and womankind)—how exactly Congress works. It's all a part of an annual, week-long seminar with Georgetown University called the "Congressional Operations Seminar" on Capitol Hill. The seminar is described as looking at how, "Congress is organized, the key players and their roles, and how the legislative process really works." In addition, it will look at how Congress affects departments and agencies in the Executive Branch of government.

The thought has been echoed that there is no reason to look at something that is never really understood anyway. But the real reason might be that NASA wants to figure out how Congress makes their decisions so when appropriations time comes up, they can better understand it. Good luck on that one.

COMPLETELY RANDOM

The Next President Is...

Let's go ahead and start by bursting bubbles for those who like to hit up their local convenience store in search of being the next instant millionaire. Not to be a buzzkill, but you are more likely to become President of the U.S. or risk being struck by lightning, than you are in winning the lottery. So what are the odds? Well, for the latest Mega Millions jackpot at the time of this writing, the odds are 1 in 259 million. The U.S. population is about 317 million, so you get the picture. You also have a better chance of being injured by a toilet (1 in 10,000) or dying from a bee sting (1 in 6 million). Sorry to be the bearer of bad news, but hey, you can run the country instead.

Baby On Board

This fact will make you realize that having a baby is no easy task. From birth to being able to use a toilet, a baby's diaper will have to be changed an average of 8000 times. That's a lot of stink. It also becomes a little rough on the wallet. 333, 24-pack count diapers would be purchased for a total of around $2,990. Add that total to the cost of formula, clothes, crib, stroller, wet-wipes, diaper genie, baby food, burp cloths—you name it—and you'll be cancelling that long-awaited trip to the Caribbean.

And You Thought Your Commute Was Bad

In November 2013, a traffic jam stretched as long as 192 miles in Sao Paulo, Brazil before a holiday weekend. Traffic jams are such common place in Sao Paulo that people stuck in them watch movies, read, and even set up dates to pass the time.

Go Ahead, Give It a Try

Try this little trick. Try to hum while holding your nose. You can't do it, can you? What comes out sounds like a whale mating call. Humming is the resonance of air through the nose and throat passages. This breathing is a form of acoustic resonance and the vibrations produce the humming sound. By blocking the exit of air, a hum is stopped.

But Can This Road Play Chopsticks?

The Civic Musical Road in Lancaster, California had originally been made for a Honda commercial in September 2008. It has grooves in the road, and when driving at 55 mph, your car will magically play the finale of Rossini's "The William Tell Overture". Originally the road had been constructed in another location, but noise complaints from the neighbors caused the city to pave over it. I guess they didn't appreciate hearing the score over and over constantly. It was rebuilt on another street two miles away from any residential areas, giving the rabbits and coyotes something to hum along with. It's a three-lane road and the musical grooves are in the far left lane, just in case you happen to be in the area. Can't get enough of musical roads? There are also some in Japan, Holland, South Korea, and one in New Mexico that plays "America the Beautiful".

Don't Even Bother Asking For a Drink

Want to take an airplane trip that takes as long as the flight attendant's preflight instructions? The shortest scheduled flight in the world takes two minutes. Yeah, don't even try to use the bathroom on this flight. The flight takes place from Westray to Papa Westray on the Orkney Islands in Scotland. The distance? 1.5 miles. Sometimes the flight takes as little as 47 seconds when the winds are blowing just right. The cost of the flight is about 21 pounds ($35 US) for a one-way trip.

You Can't Get More Useless Than This

You've probably never wondered what the dot over the letter "i" or "j" is called, but today would be your lucky day. It's called a "tittle", better known as a superscript dot. A number of alphabets omit the dot from their "i" or "j". Another interesting footnote, the phrase, "to a T," is thought to derive from the phrase "to a tittle." Don't ask me why.

Okay, This Could Possibly Be More Useless

The plastic things on the end of shoelaces are called aglets, but they also can be made of copper or brass. They are used so the end of a shoelace doesn't become unraveled. We all know how frustrating that can be to get the frayed end back through the hole of the shoe without one of these things. The word aglet comes from Old French *aguillette* meaning needle. This came from the Latin word for needle, *acus*. It is essentially a needle at the end of a cord.

Just Found One Even More Useless

The fact takes the prize for information that will get you nowhere. Reno, Nevada is west of Los Angeles, California. Take a look at a map and you will see. You can't much more of a useless fact than that.

Fun With Numbers - Random Facts and Stats

Numbers, numbers, everywhere. Numbers, numbers, why should you care? Great question, and I don't have a good answer, but these fascinating tidbits of statistical wizardry will have you scratching you head (or slapping it). So sit back as you're hit with a healthy dose of mathematical mayhem.

Math is boring, let's just admit it (okay, to most of us), but numbers that have some meaning, now those are just good fun. These are just a few that some poor soul had to figure out and count up. If you're no good in math then don't worry, there is none involved. The work on these facts has already been solved.

The average person eats almost 1,500 pounds of food a year.
More than 10 people a year are killed by vending machines.
In an average hour, there are over 61,000 Americans airborne over the United States.
Jumbo jets use 4,000 gallons of fuel to take off.
More than 10% of the world's salt is used to de-ice American roads.
It takes 492 seconds for sunlight to reach Earth.
There are 293 ways to make change for a dollar.
Wal-Mart generates $3,000,000 in revenue every 7 minutes.
Seaweed can grow up to 12 inches per day.
There are 2,500,000 rivets in the Eiffel Tower.
The IRS processes more than 2 billion pieces of paper each year.
It takes 6 months to build a Rolls Royce, and 13 hours to build a Toyota.
Thomas Edison patented 1,300 inventions in his lifetime.
The human eye blinks an average of 4,200,000 times a year.

Had enough? Thought so.

One Expensive Cup

Liu Yigian, a Chinese billionaire, paid $36 million dollars in April 2014 for a rare Ming dynasty porcelain cup that had chickens on it. What's even more fascinating is he put the purchase on his American Express Centurion Card, also known as the "Black Card", and received a special reward for doing so.

Yigian and his wife, Wang Wei, are avid art collectors, and as of 2012, had used a reported $217 million to amass an impressive art collection. In April 2014, Yigian took things a step further when he purchased the rare "Chicken Cup" at a Sotheby's Auction in Hong Kong. The cup is 500 years old and is one of only seventeen in existence in the world today. Yigian used his American Express Centurion Card, informally known as the "Black Card". The card is an invitation only card issued by American Express for platinum members who meet certain criteria, such as being extremely wealthy.

Yigian had to use the card because only $50,000 is allowed to be moved out of the country. He had to sign twenty-four credit card transaction slips since there is a maximum limit on each allowable transaction.

But what is more interesting is that Yigian, for using the card, received points from American Express on each transaction. He received 422,860,000 reward points for purchasing the cup. Yigian also managed to produce some controversy when he decided to drink tea out of the cup, as if paying $36 million for a cup wasn't enough.

I'm So Hungry, I Could Eat a Stamp

Even though the glue on Israeli postage stamps is certified kosher, it's not recommended to eat one. Kosher foods are those that conform to the regulations of Jewish dietary law, or kashrut. Exactly what is kosher can be confusing, unless you're Jewish. Meat that comes from an animal with cloven, or split hooves, or chews the cud may not be eaten. Certain poultry products cannot be eaten. I'm not sure who would want to eat these, but birds such as owl, swan, eagle, pelican, stork, or vulture are off limits. Thank goodness.

Meat and milk cannot be combined or eaten at the same time. Dairy must come from an animal that is already kosher. Eggs cannot contain blood (thank goodness, again), and only fish with scales and fins can be eaten. That cuts out lobster, shrimp, and crabs. Things that grow in the ground are okay to eat, but no insects or things with multiple or very short legs can be. Fruits planted within the past three years are a no-no. That is the forbidden fruit, no lie. This is just a short list and there is much more. I'm glad I'm not planning a dinner party.

Time to Look Through the Closet for a New Shirt

In an actual research study, it was scientifically proven that wearing a white t-shirt with a large letter "T" on the front makes you 10% more attractive and appear healthy to women. Researchers at Nottingham Trent University found that wearing the black letter "T" improved the waist-chest ratio of the wearer. It was their contention that this was a signal for attractiveness and masculinity in the eyes of females.

The study had 30 female participants that observed different males wearing a plain white t-shirt, an upright letter "T", and an inverted "T". The upright "T" increased attractiveness by 10%, the inverted "T" decreased it the same amount, and when the horizontal bars of the "T" were widened, the average became bigger both positively and negatively depending on the "T's" orientation. The researchers concluded that the wider "T" in the upright position maximizes and accentuates a man's optimal shape, making them more attractive to members of the opposite sex, while the inverted "T" does the opposite to a man's bottom half. It's time to pull out those old white t-shirts and go catch a ladies eye. It's bound to work, right?

We've Been Duped!

The postage stamp of The Statue of Liberty depicts not the real statue in New York, but the replica in Las Vegas. In 2010, the U.S. Postal Service made a major mistake when it issued the "Forever" stamp, which was supposed to be the original Statue of Liberty that sits in New York Harbor. Unfortunately, the statue depicted in the stamp is a replica that was built in front of the New York-New York Hotel Casino in Las Vegas.

The problem occurred when the Postal Service used an image of the Statue of Liberty from Getty Images, a popular online photography service, that they assumed was in the public domain for images. A stamp collector originally noticed a difference between the pictures of the real statue and the replication on the stamp. The problems didn't stop there for the Postal Service. The sculptor that built the Las Vegas statue sued the Postal Service in 2013 for copyright infringement, claiming that the Postal Service used it without his permission and continued to print it even with the knowledge that it was not the original. Since its release, the "Forever" stamp has sold over 4 billion copies and continues to be in circulation.

I Waited At That Crosswalk Forever

About 2,500 of the 3,250 crosswalk buttons in New York City don't work, but New Yorkers push them anyway out of habit. Most were deactivated by the late 1980s when traffic lights became automated. It's believed that about 90% of the crosswalks don't work. Why is that? Many of the crosswalks have been programmed with a fixed-time operation when the "walk" signal will be displayed. Many of the crosswalks with push buttons are considered "mechanical placebos" and were installed in the 1970s. By the late 80s, many of the crosswalk buttons had been deactivated. There are about 750 spots where the buttons actually work. Why weren't they removed? Mainly because of cost. It would cost about $1 million to remove the mechanisms at the crosswalks. The city decided that amount could be used more beneficially elsewhere.

If At First You Don't Succeed...

A 69-year-old Korean woman failed her driving test hundreds of times before finally passing on the 960th attempt. Cha Sa-soon, who lives in a village called Sinchon in South Korea, began her quest to obtain a driver's license in April of 2005. She started by taking the test once a day, five days a week, but then did it twice a week. She failed every time but didn't give up.

It wasn't her driving skills that were her undoing, it was the written test that was causing her problems. She had difficulty understanding the terminology. She tried the audible test where the questions were read to her but that didn't help, and she switched back to the normal test. After finally passing the written test, she still failed the driving skills and road tests four more times each. It wasn't until number 960 that she had passed everything. During the time she was working toward her license, she had become a national celebrity and was known for her perseverance. For her accomplishment, Hyundai gave Ms. Cha a $16,800 car. Way to go.

Now This is Ingenuity at Work

In 2012, a gang in the Czech Republic stole a 10-ton metal bridge as well as 650 feet of railroad track to sell for scrap metal. The gang arrived in Slavkov with forged documents saying the bridge was to be removed to make way for a new cycle route. By the time anyone checked on the gang, the thieves had dismantled the bridge and took it away. The take was estimated to be worth about $6,300, but it will cost the railway companies millions to replace. But this type of thing isn't isolated to the Czech Republic. In 2013, in the Kocaeli province of Turkey, a 22-ton bridge was stolen, as was half a bridge in India. The India bridge theft involved forty thieves who spent three days dismantling it. They had told a guard they were working for the public works department.

The Record Book That Holds a Record

The Guinness Book of World Records holds the record for being the most stolen book from public libraries. The origin of the Guinness Book began in 1951 when the managing director of Guinness Breweries, Sir Hugh Beaver, got in an argument about what the fastest game bird was in Europe. He realized there wasn't a book to settle arguments that occurred throughout pubs in Ireland so he decided to make one. A pair of twins named, Norris and Ross McWhirter compiled the first book in 1954, and an edition has been printed every year since. Guinness World Records sets the requirements on the records, and the 2015 edition is the 60th year of publication. Why it's the most stolen from the public libraries is a mystery. What's believed to be the most overall stolen book from bookstores and any other place for books? The Bible.

Are You Ready, Kids? I Mean, Soldiers?

Russian soldiers, in order to keep their spirits up during long, cold, wintery months, march to the theme song for TV cartoon character SpongeBob SquarePants. The theme song to the rather annoying (in my own personal opinion) yellow sponge, has become popular with

the ground infantry troops and navy sailors. The army captains even match their voices to the SpongeBob captain's voice when he says, "Are you ready children?" Hey, it's cold and you gotta do what you gotta do to make it through.

Nothing Like a Little Positivity

There are some police departments in Canada that thank their citizens for doing something good. They give out what are called "positive tickets". They were started by Ward Clapham of the Richmond Royal Canadian Mounted Police in 2002 as a way to thank citizens for positive behavior. The program became almost too successful as some of Clapham's officers began to complain that they sometimes couldn't get their work done because of being too popular, as kids would see the police cars and rush toward them, wanting to be ticketed. They even modified the tickets so there would be a tear-off portion as a keepsake to remind the kid of doing good, and a portion that could be redeemed for a reward, such as pizza, pool passes, or ice cream. The program continues to this day in other areas of Canada with the same goal in place of rewarding citizens for good behavior.

A Plan That Went Awry

The City of Chicago had expected $90 million dollars in traffic fines from newly installed red light and speed cameras to balance the 2015 city budget, but Chicago drivers didn't play along and racked up only $40 million in fines from the cameras, leaving the city in a $50 million budget shortfall. Though the city says it was for safety, many critics have said they don't enhance safety and are merely used as a cash-grab method to inflate the city's coffers and pad the budget. Even the University of Illinois at Chicago determined that the red light cameras didn't make things safer in a study they conducted.

It May Be Time to Make a Move

Citizens of the Principality of Monaco, a sovereign city-state located on the French Riviera, get a break on their taxes. According to Monaco's tax laws, 0% is the highest anyone can be taxed on their income. You do have to live there, but that doesn't mean you would be completely off the hook. There is a 19.6% value-added tax on most goods and purchases, and corporations must pay a 33% tax if three-fourths of their profits are not in the country. Employees also have to pay an average 13% tax on social insurance while employers pay an average of 35%.

That Was Quick

I have to wrap things up. I'll be back in a jiffy? Only if I can make it in approximately 33.35 picoseconds. A jiffy is equal to the time it takes light to travel one centimeter, about 33 trillionths of a second.

three waterfalls that make up Niagara Falls. The news spread .e local townspeople, but the news was slow to spread because : telegraph had only just been invented. Eventually word spread like wildfire that the falls had just mysteriously stopped. News finally arrived from Buffalo to explain the phenomenon and solve the mystery. Large chunks of ice had been blown by strong southwest winds on Lake Erie toward the head of the Niagara River, effectively blocking the flow of water. So much ice had moved into the mouth of the river that it created a temporary ice dam.

Everything upriver had stopped, including the mills and factories. Without the flow of water there was nothing for them to do. The riverbed was exposed, fish flopped around, and people saw their opportunity to do something unique. Souvenir hunters and curiosity seekers walked and even rode buggies across the riverbed, finding items left over from the War of 1812 such as muskets, bayonets, and tomahawks. It was a dangerous undertaking since the river water could have come rushing back at any time.

But even that danger didn't stop the U.S. Army Cavalry from parading back and forth across the river. Other people saw an opportunity. At the base of the falls there were rocks that had been dangerous to the *Maid of the Mist*, the famous Niagara Falls sightseeing boat. The boat's owners had workers bring out explosives to blast away the pesky rocks that the boat always had to avoid.

The river couldn't be held back for long and finally flowed again as the temperature rose and the ice upriver gave way. By the evening of March 31, 1848, the river was flowing and the falls were running once again. The river and the falls would run uninterrupted until 1969 when the falls would stop once more. Not from natural causes this time, but by man, in an attempt to actually help the falls.

The Falls Stop Again – In 1965 a newspaper story out of the Niagara Falls Gazette reported that if the rocks at the base of the American Falls weren't removed then the falls would eventually stop altogether. The claim was enough to prompt some action by the government. By 1969 a plan was in place to correct the "problem". The U.S. Army Corps of Engineers was tasked with the undertaking. They diverted the water to the Horseshoe Falls on the Canadian side using a cofferdam in June of 1969. It took three days and 1,264

How Mysterious Is This

The Voynich Manuscript is a 240 page, 600-year-old book that written in an unknown language, despite the best efforts of cryptographers and code-breakers to decipher it. The Voynich Manuscript was believed to be written sometime during the 16th century or at the end of the 15th century. It was named after Wilfrid M. Voynich, an antique bookseller who had acquired the book in 1912. It was believed to have been owned by Emperor Rudolph II of Germany in the 1500s or 1600s, and that he received it from an English Astrologer named John Dee. Emperor Rudolph believed it to be the work of Roger Bacon.

The ownership beyond that time is a bit murky, but the manuscript was purchased from the Jesuit College near Rome by Voynich, and was eventually given to the Beinecke Library at Yale by H.P. Kraus, who had purchased it from the estate of Ethel Voynich, the widow of Wilfred Voynich. The book contains botanical drawings, scientific drawings, and figures in many different colors. Based on the drawings, it appears to be in six sections: astronomical and astrology, botanical, biological, cosmological, pharmaceutics, and pages of texts believed to be recipes of some sort.

There is a wide-ranging debate on its authenticity. Some believe it is a hoax, while others believe it has some deeper meaning or message. One thing is for certain, it is a genuine mystery, and one that may never be solved.

The Day Niagara Falls Dried Up

Just before midnight on March 29, 1848, the mighty Niagara Falls did something it had never done in recorded history—it stopped flowing. The massive amount of water, around 212,000 cubic feet per second had been reduced to near nothing.

A local American farmer first noticed the change in the falls while taking a midnight stroll along the river near American Falls,

truckloads of fill, or 27,800 tons of rock, to stop the flow of water. The engineers used the opportunity to study the riverbed and bolted fault lines in the riverbed to delay the erosion of the falls.

The main issue was the abundance of rock at the bottom of the falls. Rock slides had caused an excessive amount of rock to collect at the base of the falls. This was of prime concern to the engineers of the project, and the main reason they had started the project in the first place. But the engineers came to realize that it just wasn't practical to remove the rock pile, and it might actually speed up the erosion process. By November the idea was abandoned and the cofferdam was blown up. The falls began to flow again and haven't stopped again to this day.

In 1973, a ballot was distributed asking people what should be done about the American Falls and its nasty erosion problem, specifically the rocks at its base. The rock pile causes the waterfall to be reduced from 100 feet to 45 feet. The conclusion of the public survey and balloting was overwhelming—they chose not to change the American Falls in any way.

Other amazing facts about Niagara Falls

17 people have gone over the falls intentionally. Five have died, including one who went over in a kayak without a life-jacket or helmet, and another who went over on a jet-ski. He perished when his homemade jetpack assisted parachute did not deploy.

The first person to go over the falls was in 1901 and was a 63 year-old teacher named Annie Edson Taylor. She did it in a wooden barrel along with her cat.

The International Boundary line for the falls was established by the Paris Peace Treaty of 1783, and later agreed on in the Jay's Treaty of 1794. Following the War of 1812, the Treaty of Ghent agreed to similar boundaries.

The foam that occurs at Niagara Falls happens because of calcium carbonate in the mist that comes from the water as it evaporates while going over the falls. The calcium carbonate mixes with algae and diatoms to form the foam. It eventually disappears and is a naturally occurring phenomenon.

The Niagara River's name originated from an early native Indian tribe called "Onguiaahra". French explorers gave this tribe the name "Neutrals" since they were peace keepers between the warring Huron and Iroquois Indian nations. It may have been for a more obvious reason, since "Onguiaahra" is quite a mouthful, but this is only an unsubstantiated theory. Either way, Niagara originated from the name "Onguiaahra", as it means "Thunder of Waters".

Niagara Falls State Park is the oldest state park in the nation, established in 1885, and landscape architect, Frederick Law Olmsted, designed it. He also designed New York City's Central Park.

3,160 tons of water flow over the falls every second, hitting the bottom at the American and Bridal Veil Falls with 280 tons of force, and 2,509 tons of force at the Horseshoe Falls.

4 million kilowatts of electricity is produced by the falls, which is distributed and shared between Canada and the United States.

Approximately 90% of the fish survive going over the falls.

How a Modern Ship Disappeared in Modern Times

Here's a news story that seemed to pass through the news cycle with just a blip, and it's about a ship that mysteriously disappeared. It's similar to the mysterious disappearance of Malaysia Airlines Flight 370 out of Kuala Lampur on March 8, 2014, in that a huge piece of modern machinery vanished without explanation. But this particular modern day mystery took place at sea.

The big difference between the two is that this mystery was eventually partially solved, unlike the Malaysia Airlines airplane that still has not been found. In this case, how did a modern ship, with all the technological advantages we have today, disappear in modern times?

A merchant cargo ship, the *MV Arctic Sea*, registered in Malta, was en route from Finland to Algeria in 2009 reportedly carrying a supply of timber worth $1.8 million. This was about the only piece of information that wasn't confusing. Beyond these facts, the entire journey of the *MV Arctic Sea* and what happened aboard are rather sketchy.

On July 24th of 2009, the ship, operated by a Russian crew, was allegedly boarded by hijackers, or pirates if you like that term better. For some reason this intrusion off the coast of Sweden wasn't reported right away and contact with the ship ceased around the 30th of July. A group of eight to ten men reportedly boarded the boat on July 24, wearing clothing with the Swedish word for police, *Polis*, emblazoned on them. The ship's captain reported to the owner that the men searched the ship and then left. The captain also reported that some of the crew had been injured. The Swedish government denied having any of its personnel board the ship.

On July 28, the British made contact with the ship as it went through the Strait of Dover. This was the last radio contact made with the *Arctic Sea*. It was believed that the hijackers made sure that the crew didn't signal an alarm at this time. The ship's Automatic Identification System (AIS) continued to signal until July 30. The AIS is analogous to an airplane's transponder. It gives the ship's position, direction, and speed, just as a transponder in an aircraft gives its airspeed, altitude, and position.

After July 30th, the ship's AIS stopped transmitting, and the ship had officially disappeared. It never arrived to the port of Béjaïa in Algeria, its intended port of call on its scheduled date of August 5th. It was picked up by radar temporarily off the French coast and seen later by a patrol aircraft off the coast of Portugal. It wasn't until August 3rd when an alarm was sent out by INTERPOL that the ship had been hijacked after the Spanish reported that the ship had never made passage through the Strait of Gibraltar. The Russian Navy sent ships to aid in the search, and Portugal did the same.

The *MV Arctic Sea* vanished into thin air for eleven days. The 320-foot vessel, a little longer than a football field, was nowhere to be seen. It wasn't like it was a fast ship either. It only had a cruising speed of about 12.5 knots, or about 14 mph, using its one diesel engine. It was finally sighted off Cape Verde near the coast of West Africa on August 14th. A Russian frigate supposedly spotted the

.vessel. I say supposedly because it wasn't until August 17, three days later, that the Defense Minister of Russia announced that the ship had been seized. The crew of fifteen aboard the ship were said to be in good shape, but for some reason, the Russians waited to keep the location and their plans for the *Arctic Sea* secret.

Things didn't become any clearer after the *Arctic Sea* was found. The Finnish Police said there had been a ransom demand, but the ship's owners stated they hadn't received such a demand. This claim was backed by the security chief of the Renaissance Insurance Group, a Russian insurance agency. He said they had been told the hijackers wanted 1.5 million Euros, and if the demand wasn't met, they would kill the crew and sink the ship.

By August 18, things got even murkier. The Russians reported that eight hijackers had been arrested; four Estonians, two Latvians, and two Russians. Two days later the Estonian Security Police said six of the eight were Estonian residents. Of these, one had citizenship for Estonia, two had Russian citizenship, and three were undefined.

The Russians stated that the hijackers made it aboard the ship by claiming they had engine trouble on their boat that was in the same area as the *Arctic Sea*. The alleged hijackers denied they attempted a hijacking, saying their boat ran out of fuel, and they were ecologists working for an unnamed organization. The alleged hijackers contended that the atmosphere on the boat wasn't that of a hostage situation, but a sort of pleasure cruise, and the crew of the *MV Arctic Sea* rescued them and welcomed them aboard.

All of the hijackers were found guilty in one form or another in a Russian court, with one man, a Latvian businessman who wasn't part of the boarding party, being also found guilty. But the speculation on what really went down on the *Arctic Sea* and why it had happened remained a mystery.

The *MV Arctic Sea* was owned by a Finnish company and was operated by a company based out of Cyprus with offices in Russia. Other than that, the Russian crew was the most Russian thing about the ship. So why were the Russians so involved in the aftermath of this incident?

The reason was because of certain rules of the sea. Under the United Nations Convention of the Law of the Sea, people charged in the crime of piracy while in international waters are tried under the

laws of the country that arrests them. Russia found the ship, so they had the right to prosecute the ones breaking the law. But why was Russia so intent on finding this ship? That was the big question, and the one that opened up a slew of conspiracy theories that didn't sound that farfetched.

Why would a group decide to hijack a ship carrying only timber, and do it in the North Sea where a hijacking hasn't occurred in centuries? Why did the Russians show such a strong response by sending multiple ships to find the *Arctic* Sea? And what was with all the secrecy? Why did the Russians take such a long time between when they found the ship to when they announced it had been seized? It wasn't until October 29, 2009 that the Russian Navy delivered the ship back to the owners in Malta. There is even a gag order on the Russian crew not to speak of the incident with the threat of prosecution if they do.

Many have tried to come up with answers to these questions since there have been no real explanations about the ship's disappearance. This has caused the theories to swirl about Russia's strange behavior during and after seizing the ship. Unfortunately, without any hard evidence, everything that has been proposed is pure speculation. One such explanation is the possible presence of Russian cruise missiles aboard the ship. There is nothing to back this up, but why did the Russians deploy a large naval force to try and find it? This theory rests on a belief that the hijackers were hired by the Mossad, the Israeli intelligence service, to stop the supposed cargo of missiles from reaching their intended destination in Iran.

Another theory had the Russian government instigating the hijacking when it found out that Russian organized crime was attempting to deliver cruised missiles to Iran, but this is a shaky conspiracy theory at best. Nuclear weapons possibly? Nope, says Finnish authorities, stating that radiation tests had been conducted on the ship while in port in Finland and nothing was found. How about Mig-31 hulls to Syria? Russia suspended that shipment in 2009, but had said it planned to deliver them.

The three mysterious days after the seizure of the ship brought even more speculation. A pair of Russian transport planes had been flown to Cape Verde to take the crew and the hijackers back to Russia. What if the aircraft were loaded with something else along with the passengers? Maybe it was the illicit missile cargo aboard the ship that was supposedly carrying only timber. Unfortunately it was another conspiracy theory that couldn't be proved.

With the gag order on the crew, and with the hijackers in a Russian prison, we may never know the true nature of the *Arctic Sea's* disappearance, or the reasons why the hijackers decided it would be a good idea to illegally board a ship in the North Sea. It continues to be amazing that a huge, slow ship could vanish in the modern era, even with our many technologically advanced tracking methods. But the *Arctic Sea* still managed to disappear, and the mystery will only continue on what was, or wasn't, really aboard that merchant cargo ship.

The Rugged Jeep

The name "Jeep" was derived from the abbreviation the army used for the "General Purpose" vehicle, or G.P. The first Jeeps were the Willys MB jeeps that were made in 1941, and they were offered commercially in 1945.

The origin of the name Jeep has widely been held that the military designation of GP, for Government Purpose or General Purpose, is how the Jeep got its name. The letters were slurred together to get Jeep, but there are other theories on its origin. The word jeep had been used early around 1914 by U.S. Army mechanics in reference to new test vehicles. Tractors supplied to the Army in 1937 also used the word, and the Boeing B-17 Flying Fortress was known by the word jeep.

One thing is for certain, the Jeep has stood the test of time. When it was first introduced, Willys-Overland, the company making the vehicle, drove up the steps of the U.S. Capitol to demonstrate its incredible four-wheel drive capability.

The History of Memorial Day

Memorial Day has been celebrated on the last Monday of May since 1971. It's the federal holiday that honors those that have died serving the United States in war. Here's a brief history behind this holiday.

The beginning of Memorial Day can be traced back to an observance of those that died during the Civil War in the 1860s. In 1868, Major General John Logan, a U.S. Congressman, declared that May 30th be a day of memorial for those who had fallen in the Civil War. This proclamation was only for the year 1868, but areas around the country continued to observe May 30th as a day of remembrance. That date was believed to be picked because flowers would be in bloom throughout the country. Logan intended for the day to recognize only the Union dead from the war, but eventually people extended it to both sides.

It wasn't until after World War I when the day was expanded to include the dead of all wars American's had been involved in. President Lyndon Johnson declared that the birthplace of Memorial Day was in Waterloo, New York, since they had celebrated the holiday on May 5, 1866, honoring local veterans who had fought in the Civil War. Flags were flown at half-mast and businesses closed down.

In 1971, Memorial Day was declared a national holiday by an act of Congress, and it continues to be called Decoration Day. In December 2000, "The National Moment of Remembrance Act" was signed into law. The National Moment of Remembrance encourages everyone to pause at 3:00 PM on Memorial Day for a minute of silence to honor and remember those who died in service to the nation.

Just prior to the Memorial Day weekend, the 3rd U.S. Infantry places flags in front of 260,000 gravestones and 7,300 niches at the columbarium of Arlington National Cemetery in three hours. An additional 13,500 flags are placed at the Soldier's and Airmen's Cemetery.

The Talk of the Mississippi

During the 1800s, the Mississippi River was a vital part of everyday commerce. It was the steamboat era and boats of various sizes and shapes transported goods and freight to ports up and down the Mississippi. Many of the words and sayings we use today got their start on the river. Here is just a sampling of a few of those and how they originated.

Hog Wash – The word "hog wash" first appeared in the 1400s and was written down by 1712. It literally meant liquid or refuse fed to the pigs. But a more interesting origin comes from the river in the 1800s when hogs that were about to be loaded were washed down by a deckhand so the stench wouldn't offend the crew and passengers. The mess that was left over was called hogwash and was not one of the more enviable tasks to complete on the steamboat. The term eventually evolved into something that was worthless or untrue and ridiculous.

Let Off Steam – Steamboats had a nasty problem of blowing up if their boilers reached too much pressure. The boats would release a safety valve to let off steam so this problem didn't occur. It's still used in this context today—to relieve pressure, or more importantly, anger.

Hit a Snag – The word snag was used in England to mean the stump of a tree, but its origins perhaps come from Scandinavia. In river language it meant a sunken tree with one end above the waterline. To hit one was going to stop a boat in its tracks and cause damage. Today we use it to indicate we've run into some sort of problem.

Barge into things – A barge is a flat bottom boat, and back in the 1800s they were very difficult to control, as they are today if you don't have a nice big boat controlling it. The noun, barge, was turned into a verb, and that's how we get the meaning—to run into things uncontrollably.

Over a Barrel – According to riverboat lore, after a drowning man was rescued and brought back on the boat, he would be placed over a barrel to force the water out of his lungs. Sounds like good fun. But another possible origin was a form of punishment or hazing where the person would be bound and put over a barrel. Either way, the meaning of being "over a barrel" is being in a dire or serious predicament. I guess drowning or being tortured would fit that category.

Highfalutin – The definition of this word is "seeming or trying to seem great or important". It was first known to be used in 1839. It's believed (and there is some disagreement here) that it originated because the high-paying passengers were on the upper decks where the smokestacks were located. The smokestacks were fluted which would break up the embers into smaller pieces that were coming out so they wouldn't cause a fire on the deck. As time passed, these flutes became fancier and more decorative. It was the either the boats with these fancy fluted smokestacks were highfalutin, or the passengers that got to stay on the upper decks were considered highfalutin. You be the judge.

Stateroom – A stateroom is a private cabin or room on a ship. During the steamboat times, the boats didn't use numbers for the cabin designation. They used the names of the states instead to designate what the room was called.

That's the Pudgiest Bird I've Ever Seen

Redondo Beach, California passed a resolution in 1983 to adopt a new official bird for the city. Their choice? The Goodyear Blimp. The Chamber of Commerce of the city decided it would draw attention to the city before the 1984 Los Angeles Olympics. The city council agreed and voted the blimp as the official bird. The city previously didn't have a city bird, and the only bird that came close was a cartoon character drawing named Sandy Seagull that was the symbol of the city's clean beach program. The Goodyear Blimp was a shoe-in for the honor.

The World's First Air Condition (of How People Stayed Cool in the Old Days)

There are times during the summer when getting in car feels like crawling in an oven. Tiny beads of perspiration cling to your head, and it feels like the seventh dimension of hell. But here comes some cool air to save you from insanity. We have the convenience of modern air conditioning, but how did people back in the day handle excessive heat? It's a burning question that no one seems to think about, and now it's time for some answers.

Turning that knob on the AC and blasting cold air so you won't melt took some amazing discoveries, and a whole bunch of ingenuity. It's been over 110 years since Willis Carrier created the modern version of air conditioning. Humans have been able to handle the heat for hundreds of thousands of years; nomads lived in the desert, and people were able to thrive in the tropics and jungles. They did okay, since as a human species we're still here, alive and kicking.

The first documented attempts at staying cool came from the Romans and their system to circulate cool aqueduct water through the walls of their homes. The Emperor Elagabalus even transported snow from the mountains to store next to his villa during the summer in order to stay cool. I'm not sure what he expected to happen other than creating a lovely pool. People in desert areas made villages with tall buildings that provided shaded paths between the buildings and had small windows that faced away from the sun. In addition, the buildings were set up to catch the best cooling tool—the wind.

Windcatchers were used to funnel the wind into buildings. There were typically more than one, depending on the building's size, the wind direction, and dust. There were three types of windcatchers. One type forced wind into the house. The tower could be swiveled to catch the prevailing wind, and the dust that was in the air would collect outside at the bottom of the building.

The second type was wind assisted and acted on a principle of the Coanda effect, where hot air moved toward a basement area where it would be cooled with water. A temperature difference was created and cool air would be forced out of the basement and out of the tower, effectively cooling anything it flowed over. The third was a solar collector that heated a chimney and caused a vacuum effect that drew air from cooler underground tunnels as the heated air rose.

The Egyptians stayed cool with evaporative cooling. They would hang wet mats over doorways. As the water evaporated, the air temperature was cooled and moisture was added to the air. This process has been used throughout history. Native Americans built water trenches beneath their dwellings and used the evaporative cooling of the water to stay refreshed. The Anasazi, Native Americans who lived in southwestern Colorado, were able to thrive by building their homes into the rock face of a canyon where they were shaded from the sun.

In addition to these ways to stay cool, hand fans have been a method of choice for thousands of years. In the 16th century they even became a fashion fad, and the Chinese were the first to develop on overhead fan powered by a person. People that traveled west during the late 19th century found that houses carved into a hillside, built underground, or made from sod, were excellent insulators from the heat and even worked in the winter to stay warm.

Modern Cooling (Kind of) – In the early 1900s, the first electric fans began to appear in homes, which provided an easier way to stay cool. In 1902, Willis Carrier, a 25 year old engineer, invented the modern air conditioner. He didn't do it to cool off people; he did it to cool the humidity where he worked in a printing plant.

In 1922, he invented the centrifugal chiller and a central compressor. The public got their first look at this new amazing device in 1925. This invention probably shaped the rest of America, even today. Cities in the desert were able to become habitable, it was used in rail cars, people were able to work comfortably in the summer, and people were finally able to cool off in their own homes.

But the spread of residential air conditioning came slowly. In 1965, only 10 percent of U.S. homes had an air conditioner. Many still used "swamp coolers" that used the principle of evaporative cooling along with a fan. While they did provide a cooling effect, they were nowhere near as efficient as Carrier's invention. By 2007, 87% of homes had some type of air conditioning. There are still areas in the world where it is scarce. The Europeans don't have it as much as Americans, and most of Africa, India, and Asia somehow continue to stay cool without it.

It is safe to say that air conditioning is one of the greatest inventions of the 20th century. There have been any number of other breakthroughs in staying cool with improved refrigerants and efficiency, but they are too involved to mention, let alone list. The entire computer age revolves around air conditioning and makes it all possible. Air conditioning is required for servers to transmit data across the internet. They have to stay incredibly cool because of the buildup of heat. The space program would never have existed, and

Google wouldn't be a company without it. It has moved our society in innumerable ways.

So when you go to twist that knob on your car's air conditioner because you don't want to break out in a little sweat, just remember what it took to get us there.

What a Stud

Chuck Yeager, easily the most famed test pilot in human history, broke the sound barrier in the Bell X-1 experimental rocket plane. What's even more amazing is that he did it with two broken ribs. But the breaks didn't occur during the historic flight, they occurred on the ground the night before.

Yeager had completed eight powered flights in the X-1 up to that point, and the next step was to take the plane to Mach .98. A dangerous maneuverability problem had been corrected, and it was felt the plane could be pushed further. The next flight would be after a weekend.

The night before he was to go up again, Yeager and his wife, Glennis (whose name had been used as a nickname for the X-1, the "Glamorous Glennis") went out to dinner at a well-known, local establishment called Pancho's. After their dinner, the couple took a pair of Pancho's horses out for a ride. They raced the horses for the barn at the end of the ride, but a gate had been closed. Yeager's horse struck the gate, threw him, and he landed on the ground. The result of the fall was two broken ribs.

A couple of broken ribs would have grounded Yeager from flying so he got his wife to drive him to an off-base doctor who taped them up. But a new problem arose. Yeager couldn't close the cockpit of the plane. He told Jack Ridley, a fellow pilot and aeronautical engineer, about the problem, and Ridley made a handle out of a broomstick which would allow Yeager to close the door. Ridley had also figured out the problems with the X-1's maneuverability during the previous flight, and here he had come up with another fix, albeit a slightly unorthodox one. Yeager was able to close the door without a problem on the ground using the broomstick.

When the flight took place later, Yeager was able to latch the cockpit before he was dropped for the historic flight. He got the plane to Mach .965 before the meter went off the scale. A sonic boom was heard on the ground, and Yeager flew past the speed of sound for twenty seconds.

Where Did "Keep Calm" Come From?

We've all seen these images plastered everywhere on the web, on t-shirts, posters; you name it. I knew it had something to do with the Second World War, but what was the history? I'm sure some of the people using the "Keep Calm" words along with some type of snarky statement have no idea of its origin. If you don't know how it came to be, keep calm, you soon will.

The "Keep Calm" poster was actually one of three that originated in 1939. They were produced by the Ministry of Information of the British government to be used as a motivational, morale boosting posters as the country prepared for World War II and the threat of air attacks on the major cities. The posters featured the royal crown of King George VI and all had a similar style. The first two posters didn't have the "Keep Calm" statement however. One read, "Your Courage, Your Cheerfulness, Your Resolution Will Bring Us Victory", and the other read, "Freedom is in Peril, Defend It With All Your Might". The third poster of the series, and the most popular today, was the one that said, "Keep Calm and Carry On".

About 2.5 million copies of the "Keep Calm" poster were printed in 1939, but it had been decided that this particular poster would be displayed only after any dangerous air raids or an invasion. The other posters were displayed instead and the "Keep Calm" posters were put into storage.

The posters didn't really ever see the light of day and were instead destroyed and reduced to pulp in 1940. The overall poster publicity campaign was deemed a complete failure as many people never saw the posters, and others felt patronized by them when they did. The "Carry On" portion did live on in a leaflet from 1941 called "Beating the Invader" that had a message from Prime Minister Winston Churchill instructing the populace to, "stand firm" and "carry on" if an invasion occurred. From then on, the "Keep Calm and Carry On" wasn't heard about until the turn of the next century.

Stuart Manley, who ran a bookstore with his wife called Barter Books, was sorting a box he had bought at an auction in 2000 when he came across an original "Keep Calm and Carry On" poster. They hung it up in their store, and because of its popularity with their patrons, began to make and sell copies of the long-lost poster. From there the snowball began to roll and other companies began to use the design on all sorts of different products. "Keep Calm and Carry On" had just been commercialized.

A UK company called Keep Calm and Carry On Ltd registered the slogan in the European Union (EU), but was unable to trademark the words in the UK. There was a push to have the registration cancelled, but it was rejected, and there is still a trademark in affect in the EU. It looks like the company has managed to get a trademark on the term in Canada, and it seems they have a U.S. pending application, but the overall fight seems far from over.

Beside from that, the poster has been used in any number of ways. Parodies, imitations, shirts, you name it, many times with the original crown being replaced by some other object. The original civil servant who came up with the slogan is still unknown. It would be interesting to think what he or she would think about the craziness their slogan has created so many years later.

A few of the remaining posters are in the National Archives and the Imperial War Museum in London, and amazingly, fifteen of the posters were discovered on the BBC's version of *Antiques Roadshow*. A woman had been given the posters by her father who had been a member of the Royal Observer Corps. One thing is for certain, the "Keep Calm" slogan has become a worldwide phenomenon.

SPACE - THAT PLACE ABOVE OUR HEADS

Better Bring a Sturdy Umbrella

Geology rocks, and on some planets it rains. Scientists estimate that on Jupiter and Saturn it commonly rains diamonds, about 1,000 tons a year. Data suggests that carbon is present in the atmosphere of the planet in its crystal form because lightning storms turn methane into carbon. As it falls it hardens into graphite, and eventually diamonds, until it hits the liquid, molten surface of the planets and melts.

Teed Off in Space

There are two golf balls still on the moon, and it took Alan Shepard three swings to hit the first ball and one swing for the second during the Apollo 14 mission. There is some controversy on how far the balls went and if there were more left up there as moon trash, but my crack research team (me) found that the evidence clearly pointed to two balls. I don't know how far they went. I've never been on the moon.

Hello, Houston?

Let's get things going and talk a little about poop. NASA has an interesting term they use when the space toilet doesn't do what it's supposed to do. NASA calls floating space poop, "escapees". When the astronauts have to do their business and the suction isn't just right, then "Houston, we have a problem." A floater can occur. But NASA astronauts go through training on how to use the toilet while back on the ground. They're even trained to align themselves correctly so this sort of thing doesn't occur. When things do go right, the fecal matter is packed up in capsules and ejected to burn up in the atmosphere.

Where the Heck is V'Ger, I Mean, Voyager 1 Right Now?

Way back in 1977, Voyager 1 was one of two probes launched by the NASA with its primary mission being the exploration of Jupiter and Saturn. It made a famous fictional return to earth as an alien cloud in 1979's *Star Trek*, as the mysterious, all-powerful entity known as V'Ger. But where is the real Voyager 1 right now?

Voyager 1 actually launched about a month after its twin probe, Voyager 2, in 1977. Both spacecraft took different flight paths and were traveling at different speeds. The probes were aided by an alignment of the planets that offered them a gravitational assist as they passed each planet. This particular alignment only occurred every 176 years. Both carried the golden records which contain sounds and images that portray life here on Earth in the hopes that some other life form would be able to decipher them.

Voyager 1 reached Jupiter in April of 1978, and it arrived at Saturn a year later in 1980. After Voyager 1 completed its initial mission of the exploration of Jupiter and Saturn, the mission was extended to study Uranus and Neptune. In 1998, Voyager 1 raced past the previous record holder for distance away from earth, Pioneer 10, which was launched in 1973. Communication from Pioneer 10 was lost in 1995. Since that time, Voyager 1 has blown past the outer planets and is now the farthest man-made object away from Earth.

Right now, Voyager 1 is 128 Astronomical Units away from Earth, or if you can wrap you head around it, 11.8 billion miles. It's currently traveling at 39,600 miles per hour, or 11 miles per second. It takes commands from NASA to the spacecraft and back a total of 35 hours to be completed. NASA announced on September 12, 2013 that Voyager 1 had crossed the heliosphere, the region where interstellar gases push back against particles coming from the sun and where these particles begin to slow. This is the last boundary before the probe will have entered interstellar space, or the space within a galaxy not occupied by stars.

NASA estimates that the probe will have enough power to continue communicating until 2025 as the Voyager's fuel for running the communications equipment, plutonium-238 dioxide, will have decayed too much to generate the required heat to keep them operating.

After that time, Voyager 1 will wander the galaxy for 40,000 years before it comes even close to the nearest celestial body, a star in the Camelopardalis constellation. Even then it will be over 1.6 light years away.

The First Space Food

The first food eaten in space was applesauce from an aluminum tube by John Glenn during the Friendship 7 mission in 1962. It was unknown whether astronauts could eat, swallow, or digest food in zero gravity. Glenn ate xylose sugar tablets with water and applesauce packed in a tube, demonstrating that humans could indeed eat in space without problems. The applesauce was sucked out of the aluminum tube by a straw and was based on Army survival rations. Glenn also had a package of pureed beef and vegetables to eat in the weightless environment—yum! None of it was deemed to be very tasty.

Rockin' In Space

NASA has a radio station, and all they play is alternative rock. The station is called "Third Rock Radio", with the tagline, "You've landed on the Space Station". David Weaver, associate administrator for the Office of Communications at NASA said, "NASA constantly is looking for new and innovative ways to engage the public and inspire the next generation of scientists and engineers." I must admit they play some pretty good stuff.

Follow the Star

The most well-known star by far is the North Star, but it's not really just one star in the night sky. Polaris, or the "North Star", is actually a set of three stars that orbit a common center of mass. Polaris A is the primary star and has about six times the mass of our sun. It's considered a supergiant. 2 billion miles away is Polaris Ab, and even farther than that at 240 billion miles from Polaris A is Polaris B.

These two companion stars are considered dwarf stars. Polaris A is a mere 430 light-years away from us, and is considered the 50th brightest star in the sky. To find the North Star, it's easiest to locate the big dipper, one of the easier constellations to spot in the night sky. If you get to the bucket part of the big dipper (where water looks like it will pour out), there are two "pointer" stars called Merak and Dubhe. If you follow the line these stars make and continue out straight from that point, you'll spot the North Star. If you get that far you've found the end of the handle to the little dipper.

Polaris is known as such a good navigational tool because it hardly moves as the other stars move around it. If you're on the North Pole, you would see it directly overhead, and as you move south, you would see it drop to the horizon. It drops from view below the equator so it's not that helpful for those in the Southern hemisphere. To use it to judge your position, face Polaris and stretch out your arms. Your right arm will be east, left arm will be west, and to your back will be south. It's not the most accurate of measurements, but it might just get you to where you'll need to go, and it's seemed to work okay for thousands of years.

GEOGRAPHY – IT'S ALL ABOUT THE PLACE

Better Bring a Bottle of Water With You

This one is hard to believe but true. The town of Calama in the Atacama Desert of Chile has gone without rainfall for many years at a time, and in some areas of the desert it hasn't rained for over 400 years.

One reason it is so dry in this area is because of the high atmospheric pressure over the Andes that causes cold, dry air to be compressed from the upper altitudes. The air has almost no water vapor and is quickly heated by the sun.

Another reason for the extremely dry conditions comes from a phenomenon called rainshadow. The moist and warm air that blows from the east, and makes the rainforests possible on the east side of the Andes, gets caught on the mountains on that side. As the air cools at higher altitudes in the mountains, it condenses and snows or rains there. As the air descends on the other side, the air warms and holds any of the additional moisture, thus preventing rain from falling to the ground. Interestingly, the Amazon River basin is one of the wettest areas on the planet, and it is right next to the driest place on Earth outside of the polar regions.

Now that's a Pool! The World's Largest Pool

Want to take a dip in the most impressive pool in the world? If so, do I have a pool for you. It's so large you can scuba dive in it, sail a boat, heck, you could get lost in it. It's the world's largest pool, and it's at the San Alfonso del Mar Resort in Chile.

The massive pool at the San Alfonso del Mar Resort seems strange at first glance. It sits directly beside the ocean and a sandy beach. Why build a pool when someone could just as easily walk over to the beach? For one, this area of ocean is cold, and it's also dangerous. Swimming is even prohibited in the area. So the resort had a problem—what can attract tourists to an area next to the beach where they're not even allowed in the ocean? The technology wasn't there to make a pool, or in this case a lagoon, the size the resort was proposing. After many years of testing, a company called Crystal Lagoons developed the technology to make a crystal clear lagoon in an inhospitable environment.

The pool at San Alfonso del Mar Resort is huge, very huge. It covers almost 20 acres and holds an astounding 66 million gallons of water. That is the equivalent of 100 Olympic-sized swimming pools that hold 660,000 gallons each. It's also long, measuring in at 3,324 feet. To put this in perspective, that is about 11 football fields in length. Now that makes for one long lap.

If the length and amount of water this thing holds is impressive, the depth is also amazing. It holds the Guinness World Record for being the deepest pool at 115 feet. Common recreation diving, for the most part, usually takes place from 60 to 100 feet in depth.

One thing that the pool does remarkably well given its location to the ocean is regulation of a consistent temperature. While the ocean just beyond its walls reads a crisp 59 degrees, the pool regularly hovers at around 78 degrees. That makes the option of swimming much more palatable, but there aren't really any other options since swimming is prohibited in the ocean next door.

The Crystal Lagoons Corporation, which designed, built, and maintains the lagoon, uses the ocean next door to feed the salt water lagoon. It relies on a sophisticated series of filtration systems to clean the water after it has been sucked in using a computer controlled system. The system then returns the water to the sea. It's an efficient system that wouldn't have been possible in previous years with previous technology. The costs would have been too high.

There is plenty to do on the huge lagoon. Go scuba diving, paddle a kayak, or even sail in a sailboat. The lagoon is large enough to accommodate almost anything. All of this does come at a price. The price tag for maintaining the pool is over $3 million dollars a year, but that is a drop in the bucket with the $1.5 billion it took to construct it. Still, a pool this size with the amount of water it has, the maintenance cost is actually quite low. Who wouldn't want to dip a toe into this pool?

The Longest Journey

Looking to plan a summer trip? Do you have a tremendous amount of time set aside and a sturdy backside? Then the Knowledge Stew travel agency has the trip for you. Come aboard for the ride of your life. The longest single, uninterrupted train journey in the world, including transfers, occurs from Porto, Portugal, to Ho Chi Minh City in Southern Vietnam, and travels 10,566 miles. It takes 13-and-a-half days to make the trip. Don't forget to bring plenty of reading material and a very strong deodorant.

Everything You Wanted to Know About the Great Lakes

The Great Lakes previously underwent the greatest freeze in over thirty-five years and 90% of the lakes froze over. People from around the region rediscovered areas that haven't been explored for years. While the magnitude of 90% is a rather mind boggling number given the total size of the lakes, there are many other amazing facts associated with these impressive bodies of water.

The Great Lakes—which consist of Superior, Michigan, Huron, Erie, and Ontario—are the largest freshwater bodies on earth, making up 1/5th of the world's surface freshwater. The lakes collectively hold 65 quadrillion gallons of water and cover 95,160 square miles. Lake Superior is the deepest at 1,332 ft with Lake Erie being the shallowest at 210 ft.

There is enough water in Lake Superior to cover the entire land mass of North and South America with about one foot of water. Not that it would happen of course, but this gives you a pretty good idea of the amount of water sitting in Lake Superior and the vast amount of area it covers. It holds about 3 quadrillion gallons of water and is about the size of the state of Maine. Lake Superior's has an average depth of 483 ft. The time when water enters Lake Superior and then leaves it is around 191 years, and it could hold all the other Great Lakes as well as three additional lakes the size of Lake Erie. Now that is a lot of water.

Around 14,000 years ago the area was covered by a glacier more than a half-mile thick. Over time, the glacier left the depressions that are now the Great Lakes. The Great Lakes have over 35,000 individual islands, and they can boast about having the largest island of any inland water body. With an area of 1,068 square miles, Manitoulin Island on Lake Huron takes the prize. There is also an abundance of wildlife in and around the Great Lakes. There are over 3,500 species of animals and plants with over 170 species of fish in the Great Lake regions.

The Great Lakes have been the home to many shipwrecks and the weather can change drastically. The waves on the Great Lakes have been reported as high as 30 feet on some occasions, being limited only due to the surface area of the lakes. The *Le Griffen* was the first known ship to go down in the Great Lakes and sunk in 1679 in Lake Michigan. The most famous ship to ever sink was the *Edmund Fitzgerald* in 1975 on Lake Superior. The Great Lakes are also one of the few places where the sheer size of the lakes can influence the weather. It's called lake effect weather, which can produce heavy snowfalls along the coasts, sometimes in clear skies.

The biggest problem facing the Great Lakes today are invasive species. One of the most pesky is the zebra mussel, named for its black and white stripes. It is believed these bivalve mollusks were introduced in the mid-1980s when a European cargo ship discharged ballast water into the Great Lakes. The mussel was already a problem in Eastern Europe and rapidly spread here. The zebra mussel is now found in all the Great Lake regions and causes tremendous problems due to its prolific colonization ability. They have nearly eliminated the native clam population. There are also over 25 non-native species of fish that have invaded the lakes, causing a degradation of the plant life and the coastal wetlands. In response to these invasive species, the U.S. Coast Guard implemented a program in the 1990s that requires ships to exchange their ballast water (which is used by ships to regulate their weight when they load and unload cargo), or seal it for the duration they are in the Great Lakes.

Here's one last fascinating fact about the Great Lakes. Back in 1996, a cyclone occurred over Lake Huron. It became known as Hurricane Huron and from satellite pictures resembled a tropical hurricane. It even had an eye, 18 miles wide.

Now to leave you with a trivia question. What is the only Great Lake entirely within the United States borders? It's Lake Michigan.

All the other lakes form a water boundary between the United States and Canada.

Go West Young Man

West Virginia is west of Virginia, right? Sorry, you would get that trivia question wrong. Virginia is actually 95 miles farther west than West Virginia. One reason may be that the border of West Virginia on the west side follows the Tug Fork, a tributary of the Big Sandy River. As the river moves south it makes a turn to the east. The West Virginia border follows it to the south until it meets with the border of Virginia. That leaves a foot of Virginia that sits farther west.

The Most Remote Places in the World

It seems as though every corner of the globe has been explored or connected with the rise in global communications, satellite imagery, and air travel, but there are still areas on earth so uninhabited, isolated, and reclusive that they have become the most remote places on the planet.

According to the dictionary, the meaning of remote is, "far apart, out-of-the-way, secluded, or distant in time." All these areas had to meet that criteria in one way or the other, but one thing is for certain, these aren't areas you can pull up on a friendly travel website.

Highest – The highest most remote place on earth? It has to be Mount Everest, right? At 29,028 feet above sea-level, it is definitely the highest place on earth, but remote? Not so much, at least not in the secluded sense. There have been over 5,100 ascents to the summit by more than 3,000 climbers. Not all of these ascents were successful, but in May of each year, hundreds of climbers ascend on Mount Everest to test their skill, and luck, against the world's tallest peak.

So what is the highest remote place on earth? You would think it would have to be the 2nd highest peak, or the 3rd, or even the 4th. No, the most remote, and also the most dangerous is the 10th highest peak in the world, Annapurna I, in the Himalayan Mountains in central Nepal. The height of Annapurna comes in at 26,545 feet and has seen the fewest climbers ascend to its peak, only 191, less than any other mountain. In addition, Annapurna has a fantastical death rate of 61 persons or approximately 41%, meaning 1 out of 3 climbers who attempt this mountain will lose their life on the ascent or descent, making it one of the deadliest remote places in the world.

Lowest – The lowest natural point on the earth's surface and also the most remote would be Challenger Deep in the Mariana Trench near Guam in the Pacific Ocean. This area is so deep that if you turned Mount Everest over and put the tip into the trench you would still have 7,000 ft between the mountain and the surface of the water.

Only three humans have made it to the bottom of the trench at 36,070 feet. In 1960 in the bathyscaphe *Trieste*, Jacques Piccard and US Navy Lieutenant Don Walsh made the descent and stayed at the bottom for approximately 20 minutes before surfacing. In 2012, film director James Cameron, of *Titanic* fame, dropped to the depths in the submersible *Deepsea Challenger* and stayed there for over two hours. There are other planned missions to journey to the deepest part of the ocean, but as of yet, none have taken place. There won't be any travel deals to these parts anytime soon.

Most Remote Inhabited Spot – The British overseas territory of Tristan da Cunha claims the title as the most remote area where people actually live on the land. This island is far away from everything and anything, situated in the center of the South Atlantic Ocean. Tristan da Cunha boasts a population of around 275 people and is 1,750 miles away from Africa, and 2,088 miles away from South America. There is no airport on Tristan da Cunha, instead the islanders must rely on fishing boats from South Africa to resupply the island eight or nine times a year.

If Tristan da Cunha wins for most remote in the Atlantic, and most remote overall, then the runner up would be the Pitcairn Islands in the Pacific Ocean. Pitcairn is also a British overseas territory and has about 48 inhabitants. A good argument could be made that Pitcairn is even more remote than Tristan because of its low population and general inaccessibility, but Pitcairn does lie near

Magareva of the Gambier Islands in French Polynesia which has an operating airport.

While Tristan da Cunha and Pitcairn would be beasts to get to on any leisurely excursion trip, one other group of islands ranks as the most isolated population center on the planet. That is the Hawaiian Islands. Hawaii is a whopping 3,850 miles from Japan and 2,290 miles from California, making it the most remote by distance, but with a population of 1.39 million people, hardly the most remote. At least on the travel sites there is a plethora of options for getting to Hawaii and you can still feel confident in telling your friends that you went to one of the most remote places in the world.

And It Really Isn't Green

Greenland is the largest island in the world. Australia by definition could be considered an island and would be the largest since it is land surrounded by water, but of course it's classified as a continent since it is tectonically independent from other continents. Greenland in its own right is huge, and not very green. Greenland covers 836,300 square miles, while the next largest island, New Guinea, only covers 303,381 square miles. Most of the island is covered by an ice sheet of 677,855 square miles. It is thought that three large islands sit under all that ice. The population is tiny. Only 56,840 people live in Greenland as of 2012, making it the least densely populated country in the world. Greenland's population is roughly the size of Pittsburgh City, California. Ever heard of it? Neither had I.

The World's Largest Garbage Dump

You would think that the world's largest garbage dump would be located on land somewhere, but that just isn't the case. The largest dump swirls in the Pacific Ocean and is separated into two separate entities by a garbage collector called Mother Nature.

The Great Pacific Garbage Patch is an expansive stretch of man-made debris that has accumulated in the northern Pacific Ocean. Its size is immense, estimated to be two-times the size of the state of

Texas. There are two masses of refuse that make up the "Garbage Patch", the eastern and western portion. The eastern portion is between California and Hawaii, and the western portion floats between Japan and Hawaii.

The ocean's garbage accumulates in these spots because of something called the North Pacific Subtropical Gyre. It's a clockwise movement of currents and little animal life exists there except for an abundance of phytoplankton. The current acts like a giant vacuum cleaner, sucking up the entire world's floating trash. Each patch is connected by a current 6,000 miles long called the Subtropical Convergence Zone which also has trash located in it.

Most of the trash is plastic which sinks, damaging life on the sea floor, and the rest either moves in the garbage patch or floats to some distant shore. 90% of the trash estimated to be floating in the oceans is believed to be plastic.

So what can be done about this giant mess? A 19-year old Dutch teenager has a proposal that is catching the attention of scientists worldwide. He won recognition in 2013 from the Dutch Ministry of Infrastructure and Environment, and although a pilot program has not been started, 15 different groups are backing what is being called the Ocean Cleanup Array. It would consist of a platform run with solar panels that would move the plastic into columns while keeping marine life out. The project would be estimated to cost $43 million a year over ten years. Costs would be offset by the recyclable plastic that would be removed.

The Land Nobody Wants

There is an area of land between Egypt and Sudan that nobody wants and has been unclaimed by either nation. The 795 square miles of land, called Bir Tawil, is the only piece of unclaimed land outside of Antarctica. Bir Tawil is mostly desert and mountains and has no appreciable natural resources. Both countries would rather have another disputed portion of land instead called Hala'ib. It has fertile soil and is a much larger area of land. But there's a problem. An 1899 border treaty says Hala'ib is Egypt's, while a 1902 treaty says it belongs to Sudan. This leaves Bir Tawil as an owner-less, unwanted piece of land.

But there is one person who would gladly take it. In June of 2014, American Jeremiah Heton planted a flag there so his daughter could be a princess. Heton, along with his family, named it the Kingdom of North Sudan and wanted to make the land a scientific test site to improve global food security, as well as a server farm for the free exchange of information. It's unknown if he'll ever get it recognized by the international community, but at least he was able to make his 7 year-old daughter a princess.

The Mysterious Airfields of Northern Mexico

A curious place exists in northern Mexico, just across the border from Yuma, Arizona. It is unknown to most people unless they've studied an aviation map. There, in the desert of Mexico, sits an abundance of dirt airfields. What could possibly be their purpose?

This oddity can be seen on FAA sectional charts of the southern U.S. that are used by pilots for navigation. There are an abundance of dirt airstrips running between an area that stretches from Yuma, Arizona to Mexicali, Mexico on the Mexico side of the border. These dirt strips shown on an official FAA chart are shown as small, red, unfilled circles which indicate they are dirt airstrips. There are no major towns around the dirt fields, and the entire area is desert. There is no other conglomeration of airfields like this anywhere in the U.S.

Who are using these airfields, and for what purpose? Are they being used for hunting trips, sightseeing, or are they just private landing strips on private land? I found that answers have been hard to come by on why there are so many of these dirt strips in these remote areas, but after interviewing pilots who knew the area, they would simply laugh and say, "What do you think they're used for?"

It wasn't hard to get the point. Many of the fields sit aside a lone roadway that leads to the border. Some sit farther away but still in the general vicinity. It was rather obvious that the fields were being used for some unscrupulous activities, probably drug running. This is pure speculation, by the way.

There was an operation that the U.S. Customs employed up until the mid-90s called Operation Skymaster. It employed informants that shipped drugs on planes from South America to the U.S. In exchange for not being arrested, the pilots became informants, giving information about the drug cartels' shipments. I couldn't find a specific reference to this particular area, but these pilots commonly talked about flying into rough dirt strips, sometimes at night, illuminated by nothing but a light running on a generator. It isn't hard to see what these strips are probably used for, and most likely it's going on today. These are just the named strips, and it is highly likely that there are many more dotting this area.

The Boneyard - Where Planes Go to Die (Sometimes)

On Davis-Monthan Air Force Base in Tucson, Arizona there is a place where airplanes go to pass into the dustbin of history, or sometimes to live again. The place is commonly called "The Boneyard", and it's home to one of the largest storage areas for airplanes in the world.

The Aerospace Maintenance and Regeneration Group handles more than 4,400 aircraft at the facility which come from all branches of the U.S. military and government. The group has a multitude of duties and storage procedures in place to handle the growing number of aircraft. Aircraft can be kept as they are and stored, making them available for use in the future, or the aircraft can be picked for parts, saving the government money (which seems to be counter-intuitive for the government). Some are even held for short respite periods, while others are sold in parts or whole. The dry conditions of the Southwestern desert are ideal for storage of aircraft and reduce the chance of corrosion.

There are many different storage areas around the U.S. for such aircraft, but the one at Davis-Monthan Air Force Base is by far the largest. The facility has processed everything from Intercontinental Ballistic Missiles (ICBM) to B-52 bombers. The facility was tasked to dismantle 365 of the bombers in the 1990s, all at one time. It was a monumental task given the size of an individual bomber.

If you're ever flying over the area, you can clearly see them from the sky, and it's an impressive sight. But many of them will never get to fly again. I know, it's sad.

The Tiniest Nation

HM Fort Roughs was constructed in 1943 during the height of World War II. It was a British sea fort tasked with providing defense against German aircraft that were patrolling the shipping lanes. Today, this same small, floating pontoon base with two towers topped by a deck is the home to the world's smallest, self-proclaimed, independent nation—Sealand.

HM Fort Roughs, or Sealand as it is known today, sits seven nautical miles from the coast of Suffolk, England in what used to be international waters. It was occupied by the British Royal Navy until 1956. It wasn't until 1967 that the fort became occupied by a new tenant, a British national named Paddy Roy Bates.

Bates was a pirate radio broadcaster and wanted to use the platform for his pirate radio station, Radio Essex. Bates claimed the fort as his territory. In 1968, Bates's claim on the fort was challenged. Bates was pushed into court after confronting men who were near the fort servicing a buoy. The court ruled that since Sealand (which was what Bates had named it) was outside the three mile water boundary from Great Britain, the area was outside of British jurisdiction. In 1975, Bates took things a step further and introduced a constitution, a national anthem, currency, passports, and a national flag for his new country.

Even though the Principality of Sealand, which sits alone in the North Sea, has been known as the world's smallest nation or the world's smallest country, it has never been recognized by any other sovereign nation. One of the reasons it has never been recognized is that the United Kingdom expanded their territorial waters from three miles to twelve in 1987. Sealand then sat in the United Kingdom's territorial waters. This created a sticky problem. Since the United Kingdom adhered to the United Nations Convention on the Law of the Sea, which didn't allow these types of structures to be considered sovereign territory, Sealand was not considered a nation.

This hasn't stopped the continuance of Sealand. It's currently run by the Bates family, especially Michael Bates, Roy Bates son, who also holds the title of "His Royal Highness Prince Michael". Roy Bates, who is now deceased, held the title of Prince Roy, and his wife had the title, Princess Joan. Michael Bates now resides in Essex, England and employs caretakers for the upkeep and running of Sealand. It isn't the most comfortable place to take up residence, even though Roy Bates had done so for many years.

Sealand issued its own currency and postage stamps for a time, and now makes money from selling titles of nobility as well offering knighthoods. Sealand made news in 2000 when they attempted to run a data-hosting company called HavenCo. The partnership was meant to be an off-shore data storage area where companies or individuals could store and serve data to jurisdictions that prohibited it, but the company never reached its intended purpose.

Many athletes have represented Sealand at sporting events, and a Sealand National Football team had been formed, even though it wasn't recognized by any sporting body. There is a Sealand National Curling Team that plays out of Minnesota, a Sealand Fencing Team that resides at the University of California at Irvine, there are ultimate Frisbee teams that participate in a variety of tournaments, and an athlete that represented Sealand at the World Cup of Kung Fu and took home two silver metals. The Sealand flag has even been planted at the top of Mt. Everest.

Sealand was recently up for sale for the low, low price of $906 million. There were no takers. But Sealand's motto is, *E Mare Libertas*, or "From the Sea, Freedom", and it sure looks like they've at least been able to continue to do that.

Derby Line, Vermont – A Town of Two Countries

Derby Line, Vermont is located in a geographically interesting part of the country. The incorporated village in the town of Derby lies directly on the Canadian border. What is even more interesting is that the border runs right through it, making for a situation where one step, even in a building, puts you in another country—Canada.

Back in the 18th century, when surveyors were drawing the international border between the U.S. and Canada, a mistake was made. The border was supposed to follow the 45th parallel, but the surveyors placed the border line north of the 45th parallel instead. This created a predicament for the citizens of Derby Line as well as Stanstead, Quebec, the town on the Canadian side of the border. The border not only cuts across the town's streets, but it also runs through individual buildings.

One of the most popular buildings is the Haskell Free Library and Opera House. It was intentionally constructed on the border between the two countries in 1904. The donors for the construction were a married couple that were both Canadian and American. Carlos F. Haskell was a U.S. citizen, and his wife, Martha Stewart Haskell, was a Canadian citizen. They intended to build a structure to be used by citizens of both countries.

Today, anyone using the library can do so without having to go through any type of border security, and there's a simple black line that runs through the building to denote the border. The entrances are on the U.S. side but a good portion of the building is in Canada. Although there are no restrictions when moving in the building, that doesn't mean there haven't been some problems. When renovations were to take place on the aging structure, permits had to be met that satisfied both countries code requirements. Everything from the plumbing, construction, and fire safety had to be congruent with the country in which it was located. The result was a renovation that took over three years to complete.

Another interesting building in Derby Line and Stanstead that was affected by the border is a tool-and-die factory built right on the border line. The portion of the factory on the Canadian side closed in 1982, but the Derby Line side of the building continued to operate under a new owner in 1988. There are places where the border runs through individual homes, allowing people to sleep in one country and eat in another. Even the water around the area makes a trip between the two countries. The drinking water comes from Canada, is stored in the U.S., and its distribution system is maintained by the Canadians. The sewage from Derby Line crosses the border and is treated in Canada. If there is an emergency in either town, crews share calls between Stanstead and Derby Line.

The citizens of the two adjacent towns have to coexist with the customs officials of both countries. Two streets cross the border without any checkpoints, although people are supposed to report to an inspection station. Anyone walking across the border, even it's just to get a couple of eggs from a neighbor, are technically required to check-in at the border inspection station. I'm not sure how much this goes on however. When people are inside their own dwellings, the rules are different. One such example is an apartment building that is cut in two by the border. The residents inside are free to cross the line inside, but if they leave the building to a country where they hadn't entered, they are then required to report their intentions to customs. Just going to say hi to your neighbor could require some pre-planning in this sleepy town.

We Have a Small Leak, Could You Send Someone?

The Rondout-West Branch tunnel carries half of New York City's water supply from the Catskill Mountains and has been leaking 35 million gallons a day for the past two decades. Even though the tunnel was designed to last 100 years, leaks were discovered in 1988 coming through cracks in the tunnel. It was originally placed into service in 1944, but New York City is finally going to have to address the problem with the 45-mile tunnel portion. Their plan is to build a bypass tunnel from 600 to 800 feet in depth with additional plans to shut it down in 2018 to complete the last phases of its construction. The leftover tunnel would then be sealed off.

But the problem really comes about when the city has to shut down the tunnel. Half of New York City's drinking water comes from this source. The city plans on spending $900 million on other projects to make up for the loss when the tunnel is shut down for eight months. Why the leakage, you ask? It's believed that the cracks started because the tunnel passed through limestone which allowed the concrete lining to be worn from water corrosion. New York City will have a sticky problem for many years to come.

How Much Do You Know About the States?

Which state has the longest continuous ocean coastline?
Alaska has the longest ocean coastline in the U.S. at 6,640 miles, greater than that of all other states combined. The largest freshwater coastline belongs to Michigan at 3,288 miles.

Which is the only state to have a different design on the front and back of their flag?
The flag of Oregon has an escutcheon from the state seal on one side and a gold picture of a beaver on the other. Massachusetts used to be

the only other state with a two-sided flag until it was changed to a single side in 1971.

Which state is home to the country's only royal palace?
Hawaii. The Iolani Palace is in the capitol district of Honolulu and was once the residence of the monarchs of Hawaii which were overthrown in 1893. The palace was restored in 1978 and is a public museum.

Which state has the longest main street in the entire U.S.?
Island Park, Idaho has the longest main street in the world. It runs 33 miles and stretches along Route 22. The longest main street without a cross street is in Potosi, Wisconsin. It runs for three miles.

Which state has 98% of the world's crayfish?
Louisiana, and almost all of Louisiana's crayfish, or crawfish, or crawdads, are harvested by aquaculture.

Which state has the most easterly point in the U.S.?
The most easterly point in the U.S. is West Quoddy Head, Maine, and it's the closest point to Europe. The West Quoddy Head Lighthouse is the easternmost structure in the U.S.

In which state was Coca-Cola first bottled?
Coca-Cola was first bottled in 1894 in Vicksburg, Mississippi by Joseph A. Biedenham. Coca-Cola had been invented in 1886 in Atlanta, Georgia but was not bottled there. Biedenham developed the process for bottling the drink.

In which state was "Smokey the Bear" from?
New Mexico. "Smokey Bear" was a cub orphaned by the Capitan Gap fire in Lincoln National Forest in 1950. He's was buried in Smokey Bear Historical State Park in 1976.

Which state has the lowest point of elevation in the U.S.?
California's Death Valley is at 282 feet below sea level. The next lowest is New Orleans, Louisiana at 8 feet below sea level.

Which state's name comes from the Indian word for "friends".

Texas. It was the term used by the East Texas Indians before the coming of the Spanish, and also commonly known as "Tejas". It was believed to mean "friends" or even "allies".

A Dubious Distinction

Vatican City, the world's smallest internationally recognized independent state, unfortunately has the highest per capita crime rate in the world, but it's not quite their fault. Vatican City has fewer than 1,000 citizens, but the throngs of tourists that visit it are the cause of a crime rate of 1.5 crimes per citizen. Vatican City has no prisons and only one judge, and criminals are usually taken into Italy to be processed through an agreement between the two nations.

THE WONDERFUL WORLD OF SCIENCE

Why Are Those Scientists Glowing?

Marie Curie was a pioneer in radioactivity research, but her research notebooks are still radioactive today after more than 100 years. Researchers who wish to view them must take them out of a lead lined case, wear protective clothing, and sign a liability waiver. Talk about hazard pay.

This Will Make You Think Twice Before Touching a Doorknob

Here's a fascinating fact that will make you think twice before you enter or exit a room. Brass doorknobs disinfect themselves in about eight hours, aluminum or stainless steel knobs never do. This is called the oligodynamic effect—the toxic effect of metal ions on living cells. Some other metals that show this antimicrobial effect are, copper, iron, lead, zinc, bismuth, mercury, and especially gold and silver. Your jewelry is cleaner than you think.

Don't Worry, It Will Start Every Time

No matter how cold it gets, gasoline will not freeze. The United States Bureau of Standards doesn't even list a freezing point for gasoline. Gasoline will slowly become more viscous at extremely low temperatures, but we're talking (by one report) in the -60 to -90 degree Fahrenheit range, with solidification being possible in the -180 to -240 degree Fahrenheit range. I think we can safely say it doesn't freeze on earth since the lowest temperature ever recorded was -128.6 degrees Fahrenheit at the Antarctica Soviet Vostok Station in 1983.

Thanks, That Was a Yummy IV

If a coconut is intact, the coconut water inside is isotonic and sterile and has been found to be successful for short-term IV hydration. This could be important in areas where there is a shortage of IV fluids or in an emergency in undeveloped countries. It has even been reported as a success for IV hydration for a Solomon Island patient during an emergency and during World War II when saline supplies were low. But don't expect to see coconut water hanging from an IV, except in some dire situation in a country without supplies. It just isn't as good as having the real thing.

Amazing Facts About Speed

"I have a need...a need for speed." These were the words immortalized by Maverick in *Top Gun* right before he did that reverse high-five thing with Goose that became all the rage in the 80s with teenagers and grown-ups alike. But what do you really know about speed? Here are some interesting facts that deal only in the world of speed.

Speed is a relative measurement, and the constant by which all objects are measured is the speed of light. Light moves at 186,282 miles per second, or 671 million miles per hour. It takes light from the sun 8 minutes to reach earth and 5.3 hours to reach Pluto, our now non-planet. To get to the nearest star to us, Proxima Centauri, takes light about four and a half years. To cross the width of just our own galaxy takes light 100,000 years.

By all accounts and measures the cheetah, like we learned in school, is the fastest animal on land. It has the capability to reach phenomenal speeds. There is a little bit of a discrepancy on how fast the cheetah can really run. 64 mph was the single measurement taken in the 1960s, and the one used for years as the maximum speed of a cheetah, but somehow researchers in 2013 were able to get a more accurate record. They studied five wild cheetahs over 367 runs and came up with a maximum speed of 58 mph. Still, not too shabby.

Another animal which can reach amazing speeds are peregrine falcons. In a dive they can reach speeds up to and exceeding 200 mph. Now that is impressive. But what about animals in the water? Which is the fastest? That title belongs to the Atlantic sailfish, which can clock a speed of 68 mph in water.

The Lockheed SR-71 Blackbird holds the fastest speed record for a manned, air-breathing jet aircraft. It reached a speed of 2,193 mph on July 28, 1976 near Beale Air Force Base. It also holds the record for fastest crossing of America. The Blackbird crossed the country from west to east in 64 minutes in 1990 as the airplane was being flown to a museum to be retired. In comparison, a flight on a commercial flight from Los Angeles to New York takes around five and a half hours.

The Blackbird did have an interesting characteristic, among its many unique characteristics. The components of the Blackbird were loosely fit together to allow the parts to expand at the high temperatures the aircraft would experience at such high speeds. On the ground, the fuel would leak from the plane constantly until the aircraft got to operating temperatures in the air. When it got there, the Blackbird's parts would seal together.

The fastest overall aircraft ever was the Space Shuttle, which would reach speeds of 17,500 mph, and it could orbit the earth in 1 hour and 25 minutes. In relation to that, the speed of the earth's rotation from a spot on the earth is 1,040 mph. And you probably didn't know you were moving about a mile every three and a half seconds. But the earth moving around the sun is going at an even greater clip, traveling at 67,062 mph.

The fastest measured wind speed used to be claimed by Mount Washington in New Hampshire in 1934 of 231 mph, but that speed has since been eclipsed by a reported wind speed of 253 mph in 2010 at Barrow Island in Australia. Good luck trying to fly a kite in that wind.

The fastest production car in the world broke the record in 2014. It's the Hennessey Venom GT, and it made it to 270.49 mph at Kennedy Space Center. The previous record holder was the Bugatti Veyron

Super Sport at 269.86 mph. You can pick up a Hennessey Venom GT for the low price of $1.2 million.

Austrian Felix Baumgartner set the record for the highest speed recorded during a freefall in 2012. He went 833.9 mph and broke the sound barrier with his body in the process. He also broke the record for highest freefall when he leapt from 228,000 feet. Just to put it in perspective, an airliner typical cruises at around 35,000 feet and cruises roughly around 515 mph, depending on the type of aircraft and wind speed.

Sprinter Usain Bolt may be the fastest runner of all time right now, but has he been the fastest runner ever in the history of mankind? In 2003, archaeologists from Bond University found human footprints in the Australian Outback that dated back 20,000 years. They determined that one of the males they called T8 was running at 23 mph. Bolt's record for running speed is 27.44 mph.

This is fascinating because the scientists determined that T8 was running this fast in mud, barefoot, and he was even accelerating before the tracks stopped. What speed could T8 possibly have hit if he had been able to run under the conditions Bolt has, such as spiked, technological advanced shoes and a smooth, engineered track? We'll never know, but it is interesting to ponder the idea.

Better Bring Plenty of Tissues

From the, "I'm glad I didn't have that problem" desk comes the world record in the event of sneezing. Donna Griffith of Worcestershire, England is credited with the longest recorded bout of sneezing. It lasted 978 days, from January 1981 to September 1983. She began her sneezing episode at the age of twelve. It began with a sneeze every minute, but as the months and years went by it decreased to every 5 minutes. Doing some rough math, that's approximately 280,000 sneezes if she sneezed every five minutes. It makes my stomach cramp up just thinking about it.

Liquid Metal

Mercury, commonly known as quicksilver, is the only metallic element that is liquid at room temperature. Mercury is a rare element and not commonly found in the earth's crust, but it is extremely concentrated when found. It was and still is commonly used in thermometers and sphygmomanometers, the fancy term for blood pressure cuff, but these items are being phased out due to mercury's high toxicity. Mercury has been used throughout history. Mercury was discovered in Egyptian tombs dating from the 1500s B.C. and was known to the Greeks, Chinese, Romans, and Hindus, complete with their own legends. The term "mad as a hatter," was thought to have originated from the use of mercury salts in hat making. It supposedly produced a finer felt. The workers that were exposed did develop twitches and trembles, but it can't be determined if this is the true etiology of the term and that these workers were indeed going "mad".

Where That Sleep In Your Eyes Comes From

You've awakened from a blissful night of slumber and feel like your eyes have been wrapped in two Triscuits. They're crusty and look like a dish drain in the back of an old diner. It takes you a few hundred blinks and a good dousing with water to clear the gunk out. You may begin wondering why that happens almost every morning, and where does that goop magically come from?

This eye discharge, or more commonly known as "sleep" in your eyes, eye gunk, eye boogers, or any other sort of disgusting name you can think of, is a mixture of oil, skin cells, and mucus, that gathers like revelers to Mardi Gras, in the corner of your eyes after a night's rest. It's also known as rheum (which would be a much more proper way to describe it), or more specifically gound, which is a watery discharge that serves a protective function for your eyes. Think of it as a garbage crew cleaning up after a night of fun. The discharge helps clear the front of the eyes of debris or waste as well as to keep the tear ducts free and clear.

You make this mucus during the time you're awake, and this is washed away by blinking and the lubrication by tears from the lacrimal gland. At night when you're not blinking, that same eye discharge collects until it forms a lovely crust along the lashes or the corner of your eyes. The watery mucus is secreted by the conjunctiva, as well as the meibomian glands that are located on the upper and lower lids. The meibomian glands secrete an oily substance called meibum that helps seal your eyes when they're closed as well as keeping tears in check so they don't flow down your cheeks. When all this stuff gathers and collects, it dries and forms the well-known "eye boogers", or "sleep in the eyes".

Sleep in your eyes is normal, but any discharge that is green, excessively yellow, or excessive when it is accompanied by pain, blurry vision, or sensitivity to light could mean some sort of eye condition or infection is present. If it's just normal crustiness, then splash some water on your face, pry it out, and get to work.

Additional Fast Fact: The corner of your eye where most of the gunk accumulates is called the lacrimal caruncle. So the next time you need to describe "sleep in your eyes", the proper way would be, "I have dried gound in my lacrimal caruncle."

Not Something to Throw Around

Acids are dangerous, wondrous things. They help us dissolve food, make products, clean things; just about everything. But the strongest one could dissolve you in no time.

Fluoroantimonic acid is the strongest super-acid known to man. It is 20 quintillion times more acidic than 100% sulfuric acid, and it can dissolve glass plus a host of other substances. This particular acid is used as a catalyst in chemical reactions for biochemistry, gasoline production, and the making of synthetic materials. It's made up of antimony, fluorine, and hydrogen. Once fluoroantimonic acid loses a proton, it begins to tear electrons from atoms.

The strength of this acid is remarkable, so then, how is it stored? It's held by our friend that we know and love when cooking in a pan where we don't want the food to stick. It's Teflon, or polytetrafluoroethylene. It has the strongest single bond in organic chemistry between carbon and fluorine. The result is a very strong chemical structure. The containers containing the superacid have a coating of Teflon so that the acid won't eat a hole through the container, the floor, your hand, etc, etc.

Bananas Can Be Bad for Your Health

Who knew bananas could be so dangerous. The dangers of slipping on the skins of bananas has been known since the 1880s, and was turned into a Vaudevillian comedy routine in the early 1900s. Unfortunately, Great Britain didn't get the memo on the inherent danger of a banana skin. There were more than 300 banana-related accidents in Britain in 2001. Most of the accidents involved people slipping on the skins. There have been no current statistics to know if this has become an epidemic.

Gives New Meaning to the Term "Fat Head"

The brain is the fattest organ in the body, coming in at 60% fat. Yes, you and everyone around you has a fat brain. The brain has about 100 billion neurons, and each one of these neurons have a thin, double-layered membrane composed of fatty acids. Right there the brain is becoming fatter. Add to this the myelin sheath (a protective layer that covers a nerve fiber, or axon, from a neuron), which is composed of 70% fat and 30% protein. Each neuron can have 10,000 to 100,000 of these connections with other neurons, with each fiber wrapped in a myelin sheath. So you can see how these numbers can be astronomical, and how the brain can be so fat. This is one time you don't want a body part to be thin.

We're Safe From the Zombie Apocalypse

The National Science Foundation paid to have a game designed where a player defends the human race against zombies. The interactive media company was awarded $150,000 to develop the game that is supposed to teach middle school students math skills

136

during real-world tasks. Why a zombie game to teach kids math? The National Science Foundation says it's needed because the average test scores of U.S. middle school children are low and students aren't able to use math to solve everyday problems. Zombie apocalypse to the rescue. Actually the official title is, "Contemporary Studies of the Zombie Apocalypse: An Online Game to Teach Mathematical Thinking to Middle School Students". It's intended to be a role-playing, web-based game where, "the player defends against zombies in an effort to save the human race." At least we'll have well-trained students applying math to stop the undead when the zombie apocalypse starts.

FOOD, BEVERAGES, AND EVERYTHING IN-BETWEEN

But It Makes Your Hands Pretty Colors

We've all heard the famous tagline, "melts in your mouth, not in your hands," for M&M's candies, but where did the name come from? M&M's stands for "Mars & Murrie's", the last names of the candy's founders. In 1941 Forrest E. Mars Sr., son of the founder of the Mars company, and Bruce Murrie, son of Hershey's Chocolate president William F. R. Murrie, had a partnership that allowed the candy to be made with Hershey's Chocolate. It was just at the start of World War II, and Hershey controlled the rationing of chocolate at the time. Mars came up with the idea of a hard candy shell after seeing soldiers during the Spanish Civil War in the 1930s eating chocolate pellets that had a hard chocolate shell. Mars eventually got a patent for making the treats on March 3, 1941.

Time for a TUMS

Feeling hungry? Head to the east coast to get your eat on. There are so many restaurants in New York City that one person could eat out every night for 54 years and never return to the same restaurant. Just in case you didn't feel like doing the math, that's about 19,710 different restaurants that you could visit.

Tequila! There's No More to be Said

Depending on the time of the year, there is a tendency for many to indulge in a fair amount of "adult" beverages. Before you consume these libations (beer excluded for now), did you ever wonder what you were drinking and how it started? Probably not, but here's your chance to be the life of the party and educate everyone on what type of tequila they're guzzling during those drinking games.

Tequila, ahh, tequila. What better beverage to talk about that has caused so many a hangover, and so many an "oops!" moment. Tequila is made from the blue agave plant and was first produced near the town of Tequila in the Mexican state of Jalisco in the 16th century. Mexican law dictates that tequila can only be produced in the state of Jalisco, with some production being allowed in regions of the states of Michoacán, Nayarit, Guanajuato, and Tamaulipas. The U.S. recognizes that tequila can only be produced in Mexico, but through an agreement with the Mexican government, bulk amounts can be bottled in the U.S. As a side-note, the U.S. regulations state that tequila can have up to 49% other liquids. That is why many recommend looking for the "100% agave" on the label. If it contains more than 51% agave and less than 100%, then some manufacturers will label it as "made from (or with) blue agave". Only tequilas distilled with 100% agave can use the label "100% blue agave".

Now, you're at the super-bargain liquor store that has eight aisles of tequilas in various sizes and shapes, what is a man or woman to do? Usually the biggest confusion arises in what type of tequila you want to buy, or what you're in the mood to do with it (if you catch my drift). Here's a quick guide to the types of tequila:

Blanco, or white tequila is usually unaged, stored, and bottled right after distillation, or stored in stainless steel containers for up to four weeks. This is considered pure, unadulterated tequila.

Joven, or gold tequila is flavored with caramel, or other flavorings and is unaged. These are usually used for mixed drinks and are less expensive.

Reposado are tequilas aged in wooden barrels between two and eleven months. Sometimes they are aged in used bourbon or wine barrels and will take on flavors from those spirits.

Tequila Añejo are aged for at least one year and will take on an amber color during the process. These are typically smooth and rich, and thus, more expensive.

Tequila Extra Añejo are a new category of tequilas introduced in 2006 and are labeled this when the spirit has been aged more than three years. They are complex and smooth.

Any tequila discussion wouldn't be finished without talking about the "worm". The famous worms are not found in tequilas, but in mezcals, usually from Oaxaca. The worm is actually the larval form of a moth or the caterpillar of a butterfly that lives on the agave plant. It was an indication that the plant was infested. The worm, however, was simply a marketing gimmick in the 1950s that damaged the reputation of mezcals to that of an inferior spirit. But mezcals are making a comeback, and many have been able to shake the image of the worm at the bottom of the bottle (the vast majority do not have a worm, but there continues to be a few holdouts that must think it's charming, or they are marketing to frat houses).

Your method of choice in the way you want to consume the tequila can vary about as much as the number of brands. If you're in Mexico, the traditional way is neat, no salt or lime. If you're outside of Mexico it could be from a lick of salt before the shot and then with the suck of a lime after. This has been erroneously termed a "Tequila Slammer", when in actuality a "Tequila Slammer" is tequila mixed with a carbonated beverage in equal parts (just so you know). If you're in Germany you may ask for a shot of gold tequila and get it accompanied by some cinnamon and a slice of orange. Oh those Germans, always trying to be different. Tequila can also be used for checkers, placed on the body, or poured from the bottle directly into the mouth; whatever floats your boat.

In conclusion, when you buy that next bottle of tequila, check the label; or at least explain why your tequila is gold or silver to your buddy who's trying to convince you to take another shot.

Yes, There Is a Difference Between Bourbon, Whiskey, and Scotch

To put it in very simple terms to start, so no one gets lost, is bourbon is always whiskey. Whiskey, on the other hand, is not always bourbon, and scotch is a whiskey produced in Scotland (and spelled whisky).

Bourbon must be distilled under government standards. By law, bourbon must be produced in the U.S., made of a grain mix of at least 51% corn, distilled to less than 160 proof (80% alcohol), it can't have any additives except for water, it must be aged in charred, white oak barrels, and aged for a minimum of two years to be called "straight" bourbon. Whiskey can age in re-used barrels, but bourbon must use new, charred, American white oak barrels. Kentucky bourbon must be distilled in Kentucky to use that name. Bourbons can use malted barley, rye, or wheat, but they must use corn as the primary grain.

Whiskey is fermented from a grain mash. This is what distinguishes it from a brandy, which uses grapes, or some other type of fruit. Think of whiskey like a distilled beer. The process is similar, but whiskey makers don't add hops like beer distillers do. Distilling concentrates the alcohol content and increases it in the spirit. Another difference is whiskey is aged and matures in oak barrels. The barrels and the method of aging are what produces different whiskeys.

Jack Daniels is an exception to the rules, mainly because they wanted it that way. It is the highest selling American whiskey in the world. It can be technically classified as a straight bourbon, but the company classifies itself as a Tennessee whiskey instead of bourbon. Under state law to be called a Tennessee whiskey, it must be produced in the state and meet other requirements. It uses a charcoal filter out of sugar maple that is not used in the production. This is the step that the company says makes its product different from bourbon. Interestingly, many of the barrels used for aging are then shipped to Scotland to be used in the production of Scotch whiskey, to Louisiana for the production of Tabasco sauce, and to Barbados and Jamaica for rum production. Another fascinating fact is the county where Jack Daniels is made is a dry county. You can't buy it in stores or restaurants in the county.

For a whiskey to become scotch, it has to be made from malted barley. It has to be aged in oak casks for a minimum of three years and must be less than 94.8% alcohol by volume. In addition, a scotch must be made entirely in Scotland, 100%—no if, ands, or buts. Irish whiskey is similar to scotch in that it must be produced in Ireland or Northern Ireland. It has to be made from a yeast-fermented grain mash and aged for a minimum of three years.

See, it's not so hard to understand. So when your friend asks, "what the heck is the difference between bourbon and whiskey", you'll be able to completely annoy them with your new facts.

So That's What I Was Measuring

This is one of those facts that end up not being all that useless. It deals with cooking and measurement. In many cookbooks (especially the older ones), the recipes called for measurement of ingredients using a dash, a pinch, or a smidgen. What was a cook to do to know the difference between those amounts? Well help has arrived. Many companies are now selling measurement spoons with the exact amounts of these terms.

The exact measurements are as follows: a "dash" is 1/8 teaspoon, a "pinch" is 1/16 teaspoon, and a "smidgen" is 1/32 teaspoon. There are two pinches in a dash and two smidgens in a pinch. There are even spoons measuring a "tad" and a "drop", though I was unable to find the exact measurements of these. There's even the elusive "dollop", but it too doesn't seem to have an exact measure either. At least there seems to be agreement on what a "pinch", "dash", and "smidgen" are, so one of life's great questions has been answered. You're welcome.

The Ever Versatile Vodka

Vodka is a one of the most popular and versatile liquors in the world, and it seems it can be mixed with just about anything. Vodka production has exploded around the world, and there are enough different types that purchasing one is like buying a used car. It might look good on the outside, but you're never sure what's under the hood.

The Basics – Vodka is made mostly of water and ethanol. Those are the basic components. You can't get a more simplified beverage. But what makes vodka a vodka and not just something that could be called a moonshine? Well, there is a difference, I guess. Moonshine is a homemade beverage, vodka is not.

There are also laws that govern what can be called a vodka. In the U.S., vodka must have a minimum of 40% alcohol by volume (80 proof). In Europe, a vodka must be 37.5% alcohol by volume. Technically, moonshine is a vodka if it is above 80 proof and not aged or touched with an oak barrel.

Leaving that point behind, vodka has been traditionally made from potatoes, but the vast majority are made from some type of grain, including wheat, barley, rice, rye, or corn. Vodka can be drank neat or straight up, chilled, or mixed with ice, water, fruit, or any other liquid beverage you could possibly image.

The History – The history of vodka can be a bit contentious, simply because no one really knows when it got its start. It's probably safe to say that it originated in Poland and Russian and parts of Eastern Europe, possibly around the 8th century. Funny enough, it was mainly used as a medicinal remedy.

It's believed vodka hit its stride and became mass produced in the late 18th century when production centered around Poland and Russia. Vodka has almost always been associated with Russia, and for good reason, they drink a lot of the stuff. In 1911, 89% of all the alcohol consumed in the country was vodka. Today that figure stands around 70%. Either way you cut it, the Russians love their vodka.

The Production – The production of vodka is rather simple if you compare it to other spirits. As said before, it can be made from just about anything, but that doesn't mean it will taste good. Anything that has starch or sugar can technically make a vodka. Grains such as rye, wheat, corn, or sorghum, as well as potatoes, sugar beets, grapes, molasses, rice, or soybeans can be made into a vodka. Even just sugar and yeast can produce vodka if done correctly.

Many vodka distillers use extensive filtration to get as "pure" of a vodka taste as possible, while some rely on the distillation and go with a more traditional approach. After filtration is when many flavorings are added or spiced with any number of concoctions.

Useless Facts About Vodka (How dare you, there's nothing useless about vodka)

Vodka does have an expiration date and will most likely go bad after 12 months. Sad but true. No matter, the stuff is usually gone in 12 hours anyways.

Until 1885 vodka was sold in 12.3 liter (3.2 gallon) buckets. Why, do you ask? I have no earthly idea. The best reason I could come up with was it was just easier and real production in bottles hadn't yet started. Don't quote me on that though.

Vodka was originally created as a medicine. It's said it can treat everything from cold sores to fevers. I guess it depends how you use it. You know what they say, "Feed a fever."

Vodka doesn't freeze. Maybe that's why the Russians like it so much since it gets cold in those parts. If vodka does freeze, then it's not vodka. Ask your buddy why he drank all your vodka and replaced it with a large bottle of water.

Vodka can be used as a mouthwash, disinfectant for razors, insect spray, weed killer, and shampoo. It can also be used for a high amount of drunkenness. I bet you didn't see that coming.

Have we mentioned that the Russians love their vodka? Drinking the spirit is such a part of Russian life that they have a word for a drinking binge that goes on for many days—"zapoi".

The Russians drink vast quantities of the stuff. Yes, we've established that. But how much exactly? An Oxford University researcher named Sir Richard Peto said that the average Russian adult drinks over 5 gallons of vodka per year. In comparison, a person in the United Kingdom drinks about three-quarters of a gallon. On top of that, previous studies have estimated that Russian working-age men die from drinking too much at a rate of more than 40 percent. Yes, you can drink too much vodka.

James Bond didn't always drink a vodka martini. In Ian Fleming's books about the secret agent, Bond orders 16 gin martinis and 19 vodka martinis.

The famous line, "shaken, not stirred," in the James Bond films has lead to some strange research studies. The University of Western Ontario in Canada, through the Department of Biochemistry, did a study to determine if the antioxidant capacity was different between a shaken or stirred martini. They found that a shaken martini has more antioxidants from the shaking process than a stirred one. Bond was right on so many things, and on so many levels.

So Drinking Is Good For You?

Not recommended, but if you're stuck on a desert island with only a few hundred cases of booze laying around, you won't have to talk to a soccer ball to get you by. Most alcoholic beverages contain all 13 minerals necessary to sustain human life; copper, chloride, iron, calcium, magnesium, sodium, potassium, phosphorus, iodine, zinc, selenium and chromium. And you thought this would be a useless fact.

It's Our Bacon, Eh?

Canadian bacon comes from the lean loin of a pig's back, while American bacon is cut from the pork belly. With that little fact known, why is it called Canadian bacon? The origin probably came from a time in the mid 1800s when there was a shortage of pork in the United Kingdom. To make up for the shortfall, pork was imported from Canada. The British used this lean loin of the pig's back to make what the Canadians called peameal, since it would be rolled in ground split peas after it was cured in a special brine. The English smoked it and referred to the food as Canadian bacon. Eventually it was brought to the U.S. and the rest as they say is history. So what if you ordered Canadian bacon in Canada? You would probably get served the peameal style of bacon. You've been warned.

Sorry, Captain. What Was Your Name?

A fact everyone wanted to know. What is Cap'n Crunch's full name? It's Cap'n Horatio Magellan Crunch and he lives on Crunch Island in a sea of milk. There is a mountain on Crunch Island called Mt. Crushmore made out of the cereal along with talking trees and crazy creatures. In 2013, someone had the time to determine that Cap'n Crunch's uniform indicated he was a commander and not a captain. Cap'n Crunch was an impostor, impersonating a captain. But who could fault the good Cap'n whose slogan was, "It's got corn for crunch, oats for punch, and it stays crunchy, even in milk." We'll let this little gaffe slide.

Everything You Ever Wanted to Know About Peanut Butter

Peanut butter is an American staple and is eaten by 94% of U.S. households in almost every combination imaginable. Of course the most common is the PB&J sandwich, but there is no end to its versatility. Here are some other great facts about that jar of peanut butter you probably have sitting in your pantry.

First off, peanut butter can't be called peanut butter unless it is at least 90% peanuts. That goes for the chunky or creamy, as well as the natural or traditional types. A jar of peanut butter requires about 540 peanuts and is the leading use of peanuts in the United States. Americans like their peanut butter and spend about $800 million a year on the food.

In addition to buying it, Americans like to eat it, so much so that they eat about 1.5 billion pounds of peanut butter and other peanut products every year. The most popular is the good 'ole peanut butter and jelly sandwich, and a child will eat about 1,500 PB&J sandwiches before they get out of high school. The debate over which is better, creamy or crunchy, is always a hot one, but creamy just edges crunchy as the most preferred. 60% prefer creamy according to the National Peanut Board.

Peanut butter was patented by a Canadian named Marcellus Gilmore Edson in 1884. It was more of a paste and sold for six cents a pound. He had developed the idea so people who had trouble eating solid food would have a nutritious and good tasting alternative. John Harvey Kellogg, of cereal fame, took it a step further, first by patenting a process to produce a creamier version, and second by touting its health benefits across the country as a new vegetarian form of food. He may have even influenced George Washington Carver (the famous developer of many uses of the peanut) when he talked about the health benefits at a lecture he gave at the Tuskegee Institute in Alabama where Carver was in attendance. It's not known if this piqued Carver's true interest in the peanut, however. In addition, snack food maker, George Bayle, is also credited with a hand in peanut butter's surge because he was making peanut butter as early as 1894.

Peanut butter is packed with lots of nutrient good stuff. Phosphorus, potassium, zinc, folate, and vitamin E, are all in peanut butter. It's high in mono and polyunsaturated fats, and is a good source of protein as well as some fiber. It can even get gum out of hair or other places! Rub some on the gummed up area and the natural peanut oil will loosen it right up.

But peanut butter brilliance doesn't stop there. If you have a hankering for a decadent dose of peanut butter, then try the most expensive peanut butter and jelly sandwich in the world. For $299 you can eat a Golden Gourmet PB&J Sandwich from Red's Golden Gourmet in Point Loma, California. It has egg brioche bread with natural peanut butter, fresh blueberries, bananas, cherry jam, bacon, and honey. Two 24K gold toothpicks, made by the House of Solid Gold, hold each side together, and they also come with their own black leather toothpick holders. Now that's a sandwich.

So if that's the most expensive sandwich with peanut butter, where can you get the most expensive jar of peanut butter? It comes from a very interesting and unusual place—the National Institute of Standards and Technology. A 6-ounce jar of what is called "Standard Reference Material 2387 - Peanut Butter" costs $253, but if you want to order them from the Institute you'll have to buy three for a total of $761. Why so expensive? The National Institute of Standards and Technology's peanut butter is the gold standard for all other peanut butters to be measured. It has a precise analysis of the peanut butter's makeup, including the nutritional composition of vitamins, fats, minerals, and amino acids, as well as the carcinogens produced by the mold in the peanut crops. Manufacturers of peanut butter use it for quality control and as a control to their own products, so it's never really eaten. I assume you could if you really wanted to shell out the money for the quintessential peanut butter, but I'll just go with the grocery variety.

Are you in the chunky or creamy camp? Keep it civil, because we all know how contentious a peanut butter debate can be.

Dinner In Front of the TV

TV dinners weren't invented because of the television. They were invented to use up an overstock of turkey left over from Thanksgiving in 1953. Swanson and Sons, the frozen foods company, had a problem. They overestimated how many frozen turkeys would be used for Thanksgiving in 1953 and were left with 520,000 pounds of the bird. A traveling salesman for the company had an idea. He came up with a three-compartment aluminum tray design borrowed from the airline industry. The company went with the design and filled the trays with turkey and all the trimmings. They even made the box look like a television with knobs. It was a natural fit for the TV dinner to be eaten in front of the TV since it kept food segmented and tidy, and was easily prepared. It was a tremendous success, and the rest is TV dinner history.

That's A Good Egg

It's a common misconception that brown eggs are somehow better than white eggs. In fact, brown eggs aren't any healthier than white eggs, but eggs in general are not all the same. The color of an egg is dependent on what breed of hen a farm has. White eggs are usually laid by the leghorn hen breed and brown eggs are laid by a breed related to the Rhode Island Red, but there are many different breeds that can lay eggs. One way to tell what color egg a hen will lay is by checking out their earlobes. Yes, hens have earlobes. Chickens with white earlobes will lay white eggs, while pink or gray earlobe ones will lay brown, cream, or even blue eggs.

The biggest factor in the perceived difference between brown and white eggs is the chicken's diet. What a chicken is fed determines the quality of the egg. Another factor is how fresh the egg is since it has been laid. No one wants to eat an egg that's been sitting around. That doesn't make for tasty eating. So if you want a good egg, just buy one from a chicken that's had a happy life.

Gotta Love Those Drinking Russians

Russia didn't consider beer to be an alcoholic beverage until 2011. It had been previously classified as a soft drink. On New Year's Day 2013, the law that was signed in 2011 went into effect, changing the classification. Beer before that time was really consumed like a soft drink. It was completely unregulated and anyone could drink a beer purchased from anywhere, anytime. The change brought a tax on the beer industry as well as time constraints on when it could be sold. It was a blast to the beer industry since beer sales in Russia had risen 40% when classified as a soda. Russians still drink more vodka than beer, however, drinking five liters of vodka to four liters of beer. On average, Russians drink about 12.5 liters of alcohol per year. That is two times of the critical level for alcohol consumption set by the World Health Organization. I doubt this new law will slow them down.

The Japan Version of Doritos

Doritos in Japan come in a variety of flavors that aren't here in the U.S., including butter and soy sauce, coconut curry, cheese and almond, and clam chowder. That's just a small list. Many of the flavors are only for a limited time. Doritos came to Japan in 1987 and the flavors that are available are almost endless. The packaging of Doritos is also very different than what you would see in the United States. One famous package has a guy basically kicking another guy in his crotch while both are dressed in a full-bodied leotard. There's no explanation for the unique packages the chips come in. The Japanese have their own, unique brand of humor, I guess.

Here's a more extensive list of the Doritos that you could find in Japan. I must admit, some of these flavors are creative, but some of them make me cringe.

Camembert cheese	Black pepper and salt
Anchovy and garlic	Caesar salad
Shrimp mayonnaise	Grilled chicken
Corn soup	Crab mayonnaise
German potato	Citrus yuzu
Smoked bacon	Grilled meat
Wasabi	Salami
Fried Chicken	Mexican salt
Coconut curry	Caramel
Korean seaweed	Spicy sausage
Sausage	Teriyaki mayonnaise
Sesame salt	Almond cheese
Steak	Pepper bacon
Mexican BBQ	

The Origins of Your Favorite Breakfast Foods

Maybe you eat cold pizza and Twinkies for breakfast. Those are not on this list, but other popular breakfast foods are. I bet you've heard of all of them, and you'll soon know where the particular food you're eating came from. Now doesn't everyone want to process that information in the early hours of the morning?

Breakfast is the most important meal of the day, at least from what they told me in health class, but we haven't always eaten what we we've eaten. A hundred years ago people wouldn't have been able to fathom the thought of a Nutri-Grain bar or liquid eggs in a carton. Here's a few of the more common items you might have seen on your breakfast table, and the fascinating journey they took to get there.

Pancakes —Ahh, who doesn't love themselves a stack of pancakes. There are millions of ways to fix them, cook them, mix them; the options are endless. But how long have pancakes been around? It seems it's been a long time, though you might not have recognized them in the old days. The pancake spans the globe and can be found almost everywhere, though the name may not be what you think. It's not really known who truly made the first pancake. One school of thought says the making of the pancake could have developed from the Christian tradition of "Fat Tuesday", also known as "Pancake Day", the day before Ash Wednesday and the beginning of the Lent season. It may have been used as a way to use up cooking fats before they spoiled prior to the days of Lent. The first known mention of pancakes in English comes from a culinary book of the 1430s.

The process of adding butter and syrup to the top is likely a modern affair with its origins coming from the recipe for crepes Suzette that was brought to the U.S. by a French maitre d' in the 1930s. Crepes Suzette has a sauce of caramelized sugar, citrus juice, and liqueur that may have started a fad to embellish pancakes with other substances.

Orange Juice – Orange juice had a simple origin but came about because of a problem. In the mid 1910s, there was an overproduction of citrus fruits in the groves of California. The only option the orange growers could find was to destroy 30% of the trees to control the problem. Orange juice would only last a few days, so shipping the liquid anywhere would have resulted in spoilage. Luckily, pasteurization came to the rescue and was discovered. It, along with the national railway system being in place, allowed orange juice to be shipped across the country, pleasing orange juice drinkers nationwide.

Wheaties – I think I've had only one bowl of Wheaties in my life, mainly because I was busy eating too many Fruit Loops, but the story behind them is pretty good. In 1922, a worker for the Washburn Crosby Company, which would later become General Mills, accidentally spilled a wheat bran mixture on a hot stove. Yup, that's it, and I wonder who took the first taste to see if it tasted like anything. It took 36 attempts to get the flakes strong enough to survive packaging, and by 1924 they had done it. The name was originally Washburn's Gold Medal Whole Wheat Flakes (sounds yummy) but was changed to Wheaties after an employee contest to name the product.

Its first association with the sporting world began in 1927 at a minor league baseball park in Minneapolis, Minnesota. A new slogan was written by Knox Reeves, an adman from a Minneapolis ad agency, and he came up with the words, "Wheaties-Breakfast of Champion". In the 1930s, athlete testimonials spurred the cereal on and the company began using them on the packaging. Michael Jordan has appeared on the Wheaties box the most at 18 times with Tiger Woods second at 14.

Pop-Tarts – Kellogg Pop-Tarts are as American as apple pie. Whether you love 'em or hate 'em, they are a breakfast food force. As I've explained before, they're even popular during hurricanes, where strawberry Pop-Tarts were the top selling item at Wal-Mart along with beer.

Beer and Pop-Tarts are a wonderful mix, but how did Por-Tarts get their start? The company that really started it was Post, the cereal maker. In 1963, Post had found a way to keep fruit filling fresh without a refrigerator, and they were set to dominate the breakfast food market. But they made a grave error, they announced the product before it was ready to be sold. Kellogg swooped in and took the idea and ran with it in under six months. They had it placed in the baking aisle, strategically away from the cereals, and named it Pop-Tart, a ode to the pop art movement. The original flavors were strawberry, apple-currant, blueberry, and brown sugar cinnamon. The frosted versions didn't arrive for three more years as Kellogg had to get the frosting to stay on the tart. Kellogg has released 29 other versions of Pop-Tarts since that time.

Coffee – Okay, so coffee in itself has a been around for a really long time. Its origins can be traced to around 800 A.D. in Ethiopia and an interesting legend about an Ethiopian goat herder named Kaldi. Coffee is said to have gotten its real start in Arabia where beans were roasted around 1000 A.D. and where no coffee beans were have said to have left the area until the 1600s. It next spread to Europe where it was introduced in Venice in 1615.

But everyone wanted in on the coffee game. The Dutch managed to smuggle a plant into Europe, and not just the beans, in 1616. They later set up their own coffee estate in colonial Java, which is now part of Indonesia. The French came up next around

1714, and due to a French naval officer named Gabriel Mathieu De Clieu, who was able to get clippings from King Louis XIV's coffee tree, (without his permission of course), set sail with them for Martinique, a French colony in the Caribbean. After a storm, pirates, and an overall horrible journey, De Clieu managed to plant his cutting in Martinique. That single plant ended up yielding about 18 million trees in about 50 years. That plant's offspring would make up the coffee plants that would eventually spread around Latin America.

In 1727, it was Brazil's turn, and they performed another bit of coffee high jinks. Lt. Col. Francisco de Melo Palheta of Brazil went on a mission to smuggle coffee seeds from French Guiana. He somehow got the governor's wife to give him some seeds, which were cleverly disguised in a bouquet that she had presented to him at a farewell dinner. These few seeds made Brazil into a coffee empire by the 1800s, allowing coffee to be enjoyed by the masses.

Doughnuts or Donuts (whichever you prefer) – The origin of the doughnut can be traced in one form or another to prehistoric Native American times, but its real origins are murky. The doughnut is believed to have appeared in New Amsterdam, a Dutch settlement which is now Manhattan, in the 1800s and were known as "oily cakes", or "olykoeks". But since the most distinct portion of a doughnut is its hole, where did that come from?

Again history is slightly murky on the subject, but an American named Hanson Gregory claimed credit for putting the hole in the doughnut. His mother is believed to have come up with the name doughnut when she made a pastry treat for him, and the ship's crew he was with, to eat during long voyages. She made them a deep-fried dough that had walnuts or hazelnuts in the center. Gregory was said to have put the hole there by using the top of a round tin pepper box, pushing the contents from the center.

So if Gregory reportedly made the hole, how did they end up becoming so popular? That can be traced to World War I, where American soldiers (also known as doughboys, but that didn't have anything to do with doughnuts. It came from the Civil War) fought in the trenches. They were served doughnuts by women volunteers who had brought them to give the soldiers a taste of home. When those soldiers returned home, they had a hankering for the fried treat. In 1920, doughnut making hit its stride when a refugee from Russia named Adolph Levitt built the first doughnut making machine. Levitt's doughnut machines ended up making him $25 million a year, and by the time of the 1934 Chicago's World's Fair, doughnuts were known as the "food hit of the Century of Progress". Doughnuts were being consumed by the masses, regardless of their socioeconomic status.

It was also in the 30s when Joe LeBeau, a Frenchman, sold his secret recipe to Ishmael Armstrong, a store owner in Paducah, Kentucky. That recipe and the name that went with it was called Krispy Kreme. Other entrepreneurs started on their path to the doughnut fortune as Krispy Kreme grew. Dunkin' Donuts started in 1950 in Quincy, Massachusetts and today has stores in 37 countries, as well as having double the amount of stores in the U.S. as Krispy Kreme. Doughnuts are far from losing any steam in popularity. It's estimated that overall production of doughnuts in the U.S. is around 10 billion doughnuts every year.

Eggos – These frozen waffles were invented in San Jose, California in 1953 by three brothers, Tony, Sam, and Frank Dorsa. They were originally known as "Froffles", a concocted name from "frozen waffles". People began to refer to them as Eggos due to their egg-like taste, and the brothers changed their name to the Eggo Brothers. Kellogg bought their company in 1968 and were the ones to come up with the popular, "L'eggo my Eggo," advertising campaign.

Egg McMuffin – In 1970, Jim Delligatti, a McDonald's franchisee who had developed the Big Mac, was looking for additional ways he could bring in more patrons for breakfast to his restaurant. He began by selling the usual early morning items of coffee and doughnuts. He later added pancakes and sausage. While Delligatti was doing well during his morning hours, other McDonald's operators didn't have the same wish to open earlier for breakfast, unless there was something that could really rocket sales.

In 1971, a new franchisee named Herb Peterson also saw the opportunity that serving breakfast could bring. He decided to come up with a product that was like other products on the McDonald's menu and one that could be eaten by hand. He came up with a cluster of six rings that formed an egg into the shape of an English muffin. He then added a piece of Canadian bacon to finish it off. Ray

Kroc, the founder of McDonald's, signed off on the new product almost as soon as he had tasted it. By 1976, McDonald's had finely tuned their breakfast menu, way before others jumped on the breakfast bandwagon in the mid 1980s.

So before you chomp down on your next breakfast, take a little time to think where it came from. It took many events to happen so we can have the breakfast we know today. Now go enjoy your piece of cold pizza.

So That's What We've Been Eating

Craisins, made by Ocean Spray, are not actually dried, shriveled, whole cranberries, but are made from cranberry husks that are reinfused with juice. The cranberry husks used to be thrown away by farmers until Ocean Spray came up with the process. And Ocean Spray hasn't stopped there. They've released a juice-infused version with cherry, blueberry, or pomegranate juices. If that wasn't enough, they've even added a fruit cluster version, trail mix Craisins, Greek yogurt covered Craisins, and to top it off, chocolate covered Craisins. The raisin industry is not too happy with the development, we're sure.

But Craisins aren't the only thing that has possibly been reinvented by Ocean Spray. Another byproduct of their juicing process could end up being used elsewhere. At Ocean Spray's juice processing facilities, shredded cranberry skins, called pomace, are taken away to the landfill. Research is being done to see if the waste could be used as an additive for soil in growing plants, allowing the shredded skins to be used for gardening instead of going to the landfill.

Beef Country

As of 2015, the world's largest exporter of beef was surprisingly the country of India. Yes, India, where the cow is sacred and revered due to the Hindu culture. But it's probably not the beef you're thinking of. The country exports large amounts of water buffalo, mainly to North Africa, Asia, and the Middle East. The top beef exporters after India were more of who you would expect. Brazil was second, Australia was third, and the U.S. was fourth.

AND THAT'S THE END

I hope you enjoyed the first volume of *Knowledge Stew: The Guide to the Most Interesting Facts in the World*, and either learned some new facts, or strengthened your overall knowledge of the world around you. Feel free to pop over to the website to see what's cooking in the stew pot at knowledgestew.com.

Thanks again for reading. Be sure to enlighten everyone around you with any of the new things you've learned. They'll appreciate you for it.

Sincerely,

Daniel Ganninger

ABOUT THE AUTHOR

Daniel Ganninger lives with his wife and two children in Central Texas and has a love of trivia and flying airplanes. He graduated from the University of Texas and when not writing works at his other profession in the medical field. He has written five books in the *Icarus Investigations* mystery series, along with the current *Knowledge Stew* guide. You can find out what he's working on next, or to join the newsletter, visit his website at www.danielganninger.com.

Look for Volume 2 and Volume 3 of the next *Knowledge Stew: The Guide to the Most Interesting Facts in the World*.

Visit the website where everything started at **Knowledgestew.com**

More Books by Daniel Ganninger:

The fun, humorous, mystery and adventure, *The Case Files of Icarus Investigations*:

Flapjack, Case File #1
Peeking Duck, Case File #2
Snow Cone, Case File #3
Coconut Water, Case File #4
Stolen Dough Case File #5
Bitter Pill Case File #6
Micro Wave Case File #7 - Coming Soon

Made in the USA
Middletown, DE
23 December 2016